WITH CLOUGH
BY TAYLOR

PETER TAYLOR

WITH MIKE LANGLEY

WITH CLOUGH BY TAYLOR

Biteback Publishing

This edition published in Great Britain in 2019 by
Biteback Publishing Ltd
Westminster Tower
3 Albert Embankment
London SE1 7SP
Copyright © Peter Taylor and Mike Langley 1980, 2019

ISBN 978-1-78590-455-4

10 9 8 7 6 5 4 3 2 1

A CIP catalogue record for this book is available from the British Library.

Set in Adobe Caslon Pro

Printed and bound in Great Britain by
CPI Group (UK) Ltd, Croydon CR0 4YY

MIX
Paper from
responsible sources
FSC® C020471

For Lilian, Wendy and Philip
With thanks for their honesty and support through all seasons

ACKNOWLEDGEMENTS

Particular thanks for guidance and assistance to Reg Drury, Gerald Mortimer and Mrs Daphne Blanch.

CONTENTS

FOREWORD BY
WENDY DICKINSON

I first realised that my dad didn't have an ordinary job at the age of six or seven. At school one day in Middlesbrough the chat turned to what our dads did for a living – nobody asked what your mum did in those days. The usual 'normal' jobs were revealed, but when I said my dad played football my friends just burst out laughing. 'That's not a proper job,' said one. 'That's just messing about.'

At that time – the late 1950s – he was 'messing about' as a goalkeeper for Middlesbrough FC, where he formed an instant bond with a young centre-forward. My late mum, Lilian, recalled Dad coming home from training after having been at the club for a couple of weeks, excited about an amazing young footballer he'd met. 'What's his name?' asked Mum.

'Brian Clough,' was the answer. Little did any of us know what a momentous meeting that would prove to be.

As a little girl, I remember Brian coming to our house regularly. When my brother Phil was born in 1957, Brian's mam arranged the christening as she was horrified that my atheist dad wasn't planning on one. Brian and his sister, Deanna, were the godparents.

Clough and Taylor's lives were intertwined for only a few short years as players, but they were inseparable; even the Middlesbrough FC team photo has them standing shoulder to shoulder. The glue that bound them was a shared passion for how the game should be played and an ill-concealed disdain for those who didn't share their vision.

In 1961 they went their separate ways – Brian to Sunderland and a career-ending injury and Dad to his first managerial job at Burton Albion. Four years later, a call from Brian – soon to become the youngest manager in the Football League at Hartlepools United – sent our little family back up north, where Dad became Brian's assistant.

They went on to build stunning teams at Derby County and Nottingham Forest and their place in the football history books was guaranteed.

One question people always ask me about Clough and Taylor is why they broke up. In true 'dynamic duo' style, the end proved to be as spectacular as the partnership. They fell out and both passed away without exchanging another word. You couldn't make it up.

But the aforementioned history books can explain all about that. What I can tell you, as a daughter and a friend, is that all who shared in the journey with Clough and Taylor were privileged to be there. It was truly heart-stopping and, if you were lucky enough to be in the same room when they were on a roll, you'd never forget it.

Phil and I have discussed the breakup on more than one occasion with Brian's sons, Simon and Nigel. We all agree that they were stupid and should both have picked up the phone, but I never dwell on that because the great times were far more important. In truth, bearing in mind that they were both such strong-minded, opinionated men, I am more surprised that they managed to stay together so long.

We were lucky to have them and to have been part of their amazing lives, and I thank my lucky stars that I was there.

Dad died aged just sixty-two, on 4 October 1990, of idiopathic pulmonary fibrosis. This cruel disease, which causes scarring of the lungs, has no known cause or cure. The average life expectancy following diagnosis is just three to five years. Phil and I have asked for royalties from the book to be donated to the charity Action for Pulmonary Fibrosis. www.actionpulmonaryfibrosis.org.

CHAPTER 1

THE START OF OUR PARTNERSHIP

The voice of Brian Clough has been likened to the sound of rending calico, but it can also be as rousing as a bugle call and change people's lives, as it did mine in the autumn of 1965.

Holiday postcards excepted, I hadn't heard from Brian in four years until he telephoned my home and came straight to the point.

'I've been offered the managership of Hartlepools and I don't fancy it. But if you'll come, I'll consider it.' Then he banged the phone down.

Can there ever have been a more offhand summons to football glory? For that was the birth, or rather the conception, of a partnership destined to win the League Championship for both Derby County and Nottingham Forest, to spend millions of pounds on players while smashing transfer records, to win the Football League Cup twice, to win at Wembley and to win the European Cup twice. Enemies dubbed us 'the Kray twins', an insulting label in which the only grain of truth is the twin-like affinity of our views on how to run a successful club; we have fought, argued and even split up for a couple of years, but have never differed on this basic conviction.

The phone call about the job at Hartlepools, however, caught me in a quandary, for I was already a successful manager with Burton Albion in the Southern League. I had just moved into a bungalow with my wife Lilian and our children Wendy and Philip; I had a three-year contract at £34 a week, as well as a perk of £7 a week for coaching at a high school. The club were top of the table and recent winners of the Southern League Cup when Brian rang; because he hung up without giving me time to speak, I had to call him back and explain the position.

'I've only had this three-year contract for a few days and I'm very proud of it, but at the same time I'm mad keen to get into the Football League. Can we meet halfway and discuss it?' He said, 'I'll see you in York.' We settled on the Chase Hotel by the racecourse; I went with Lilian and he arrived with his wife, Barbara, and their young son, Simon, in his arms. He wasn't the spruce, boyish Brian Clough I had known at Middlesbrough. His face reflected a dreadful year in which he had been sacked as Sunderland's youth coach and warned by medical specialists that he must never play serious football again.

'No one knows how hard that hit me,' he confessed later. 'I went berserk for a time, drinking heavily and being hell to live with.' He didn't need to tell me. I saw the drink in his thickened features and realised he had reached a dead end in his career.

His testimonial match later that month was expected to raise at least £5,000, but money would not cure his problems. He needed work, even at such a hopeless club as Hartlepools. 'I don't fancy the place,' he said. 'Still less do I fancy the man who is offering the job. But I can't go on as I am.'

Brian was recommended to Hartlepools by the former Sunderland and England inside-forward, Len Shackleton, the north-east sports columnist for the *Sunday People*. The directors had been convinced by Shackleton that their club would run better under two bosses, and he then persuaded Brian to approach me.

Shackleton had hit upon an idea that had been in my mind for years; the belief that two men – the right two – could build up a club quicker than one. Brian and I complemented each other; we got on well together and were particularly alike in wanting results quickly.

'You'll be my right hand,' said Brian. 'Not an assistant manager, more a joint manager, except that they don't go in for titles at Hartlepools and we'll have to disguise you as the trainer. The other bad news is that they can't afford to pay you more than £24 a week.'

It meant dropping £17 a week, enough then to pay the mortgage on a house. I would be dropping in status from manager to trainer. It meant running out with the sponge on match days, a job that I dislike. It meant going against the advice and wishes of my wife and closest friends, who wanted me to stay at Burton where, if my cup victory was followed by promotion from our division of the Southern League, I would be qualified for a Football League club of my own.

Yet, against all logic, I promised Brian, 'I'll come.' We shook hands on it, and that's how we started.

CHAPTER 2

PLAYING DAYS

Brian Clough scored 200 league goals in 219 games. No one has done it faster and probably never will.

I first met Brian at Middlesbrough in 1955; he was freshly demobbed from the Royal Air Force and I was the new reserve goalkeeper, signed for £3,500 from Coventry City. I cannot remember laying eyes on him until the second half of the traditional pre-season fixture. Probables *v.* Possibles. He was the fourth centre-forward to be tried and I was impressed immediately by the way this crew-cut unknown shielded the ball and how cleanly he struck it. Above all, I admired the arrogance of his play.

Back in our dressing room, I began asking, 'Who was that young fellow who came on last for them?' But no one seemed to know or care. Brian was lost in a crowd of more than thirty full-time players. 'Some lad from the RAF,' they said.

Middlesbrough had signed him in September 1952, for the minimum registration fee of £10. He was a sixteen-year-old with a North Yorkshire village side called Broughton Rangers, whose ranks were full of Cloughs because his brothers Joe, Des and Billy were also in the team.

The scout was George Camsell, an England centre-forward who scored a record 326 league goals for Middlesbrough up to the outbreak of the Second World War. Camsell knew a goal-machine when he saw one, but the people who ran the club didn't. Brian was rated so lightly that the club never bothered fetching him home to play at Ayresome Park during his two years of national service, which were spent mostly at Watchet in Somerset. He played there for the station team without progressing to the full RAF team for the inter-services championship. When I joined Middlesbrough, he was only the fourth choice centre-forward.

Clubs in those days signed lads by the busload, often using hardly any judgement and with no aim beyond preventing rivals from snatching a starlet off their doorstep. A tenner changed hands and the boy was usually forgotten, although tied for life to a Football League form. That might have been Brian's fate, too, but for his initiative in writing a reminder to Middlesbrough just before his demobilisation. 'I asked them to take me on, they didn't ask me,' he said to me about his start in professional football.

He had been a month at Ayresome Park when I arrived, training with more than thirty full-time players. It was a huge staff for a modest Second Division club and I saw why manager Bob Dennison had talked of pruning the dead wood when he signed me as the eventual replacement for Middlesbrough's spectacular goalkeeper Rolando Ugolini. I signed on August Bank Holiday – the first Monday of the month in those days – and trained through my first week, unaware of the existence of Brian Howard Clough until that second half of the Probables *v.* Possibles.

Charlie Wayman, a veteran who remained a clever footballer, was Middlesbrough's number one choice. His deputy was Ken McPherson, who had been bought from Notts County for £18,000, which was a high fee in those days. After McPherson, they trotted out a local lad called Doug Cooper, who, in fact, went on to start the season with the first team. Then this unknown number nine appeared and registered with me immediately.

I've never been backward about voicing my opinions. When I suggested, 'That lad can't half play,' the other players merely shrugged, but Brian himself sidled up after a while. Someone had told him that I was singing his praises and that was how our friendship began. Brian, once I had singled him out for stardom, was always by my side. He would knock at my door five or six nights a week and sit around there or

7

in Rea's Ice Cream Parlour talking football, never tiring of hearing me say that he would become a great player. Rea's in those days was the players' headquarters and fans said the team was picked there.

I welcomed him because I was a stranger in a dull town. Middlesbrough of the mid-'50s was a place where hundreds of men shuffled on the pavements of the main street on Sunday mornings, gazing expectantly at the town hall clock. At the first stroke of noon, they tensed like runners on a starting line. By the twelfth stroke, they had vanished into the opening doors of pubs. What drab pubs, too – many were sawdust-on-the-floor alehouses that refused admission to women.

Emptying pint pots seemed the chief preoccupation of Middlesbrough's shipyard workers and steelmen; after that came football, horses, dogs and pigeons. They voted solidly for Labour but, outside elections, spared few thoughts for politics. I remember taking Brian to hear Harold Wilson, then the rising star of the Labour Party, at a working men's club one Sunday afternoon. The audience numbered barely fifty. I was politically conscious in those days but grew disillusioned, while Brian – despite taunts of 'Rolls-Royce communist' from fellow managers – remained a socialist.

I may have influenced him in that way, as I did in many others, by coming into his life when he was seeking a guiding light. I was six years older, married, a father and experienced in professional football. He was attracted by my faith in him; I was attracted by his unerring ability to put the ball in the net.

We had more than football in common. Our backgrounds were similar, both coming from large families. I was one of eight children and Brian was one of nine, eight of them still living. I saw my own parents in his – Sarah, his mother, whom everyone called 'Sal', and Joe, his father, who worked in a sweets factory near the football ground. They ran the Cloughs with precision; punctuality was their rule and the house was spotless.

Brian and I played together for the first time only a week after the Probables *v.* Possibles match. We were in Middlesbrough's reserves at Spennymoor and the director in charge – a Mr Winney, who later became the club chairman – gave us an uplifting talk about our opportunities for promotion to the first team, not realising that the management and staff were blind to the diamond under their noses. They ought to have given Brian an immediate place in the first team; instead, they were giving him adverse reports such as, 'Doesn't work hard enough on the field.' The author was Jimmy Gordon, a Scottish wing-half who coached Brian at Ayresome Park and was later to work for him as a trainer-coach at Derby County, Leeds United and Nottingham Forest.

I decided to take the future of Brian Clough into my own hands by contacting a manager whose soul will march on as long as Brian and I remain in football. The credit for founding the partnership of Clough and Taylor belongs to Len Shackleton, but we are indebted for our creed to an unusual old man called Harry Storer, who was my boss for a time at Coventry City.

Coventry had signed me as a professional at seventeen after I had played twice as an amateur for Nottingham Forest's first team against Notts County, a home-town derby for me in the wartime league. I went to Coventry as a part-timer because my father insisted on the completion of my apprenticeship to bricklaying, a trade that I had in common with such managers as Bob Paisley of Liverpool and Tony Book of Manchester City.

I was with Coventry for nine years before I was sold to Middlesbrough; I was eager to go because the writing was on the wall in the shape of Reg Matthews, a young goalkeeper of such phenomenal ability that England capped him the following year while he was still only a Third Division player. I saw Matthews as a schoolboy and recognised him as a probable international, which meant there would be no hope for me once he was old enough for the first team.

Jesse Carver, who had been a successful manager in Italy with FC Roma, had just taken over at Coventry with a new coach, George Raynor, a knowledgeable little man who became famous a few years later by guiding Sweden to the 1958 World Cup final against Brazil. Footballers trained like racehorses in those days, slogging endlessly round the running track. At some English clubs, the players never saw a ball from Saturday to Saturday because of managers who believed, 'If you see too much of the ball during the week you won't be hungry for it in matches.' Carver and Raynor, though, thought like Continentals and concentrated their training on ball skills and positional technique. I spent an enlightening fortnight under them before joining Middlesbrough. Nevertheless, it was Harry Storer whom I decided to ring.

No one at Middlesbrough ever guessed how close Brian came to being Storer's player. I fixed up a deal and Harry, until his dying day, never ceased to reproach himself for not pushing it through.

Storer was fifty-seven years old and coaching cricket at a Butlin's holiday camp when Derby County, who had been relegated to the old Third Division (North), recalled him to football managership in 1955. Only one club, not three, was promoted in those days, but he put them back in the Second Division in two seasons. Derby were due to visit the north-east early in September for a match at Hartlepools so I phoned Harry saying, 'I'd like you to meet the best young centre-forward I've ever seen.' 'Meet me at the Hartlepools ground,' he said, and when we arrived, 'Let's go on the pitch where we won't be overheard.'

The two of us walked to the centre circle. Brian stayed by the touchline and never opened his mouth. He either didn't understand or was unable to believe that, doubtless in flagrant violation of league regulations, his new friend and a famous manager could be standing in broad daylight plotting his transfer to Derby County while he was still only the fourth choice at his own club.

'You can have him for peanuts,' I told Harry. 'The staff at Middlesbrough reckon he's not mobile enough.'

'Has he got enough off?' asked Harry, referring to the level of Brian's skill when coming away from defenders to collect the ball near midfield.

'As much as he needs.'

Harry persisted, 'Can he receive it and lay it and keep the line going?'

'Yes,' I said, 'although his strength is in and around the box.' Storer thought about it. 'He'll do, if you say so. But I've just blown my cash by buying Martin McDonnell [a hard centre-half] and Paddy Ryan [a lively inside-forward].'

'But you'll get Brian Clough for nothing. They don't rate him.'

'Sorry, but I haven't a bean' – a sentence that haunted him once Brian began rattling in the fastest 200 goals ever scored in the Football League. 'What a tragedy,' Harry often groaned to me. 'If only I'd had some money.' I refused to let him off the hook.

'You didn't need money. Brian was available, practically as a give-away. All you had to do was ask.'

Ten days after meeting Storer, and against all the indications, Brian made his league debut on 17 September 1955 against Barnsley. He didn't establish himself and was picked for only nine games that season, scoring three goals. I played only six league games myself and the pair of us were regarded as no more than useful reserves – underpaid reserves, in his case.

Brian still lived at home and mentioned one evening, 'I'm finding it hard to manage after giving my keep to Mam.' He showed me his pay slip; after stoppages, Middlesbrough were paying him £11 and a few pence for a fortnight. 'I can earn more labouring in ICI,' he said.

'Don't talk that way. You're not quitting, you are going to get paid what you're really worth.' I briefed him on what a Second Division reserve ought to expect as wages; the next day he put his case to the club and won an increase of £2 10 shillings a week.

Today, when star players earn more than £1,000 a week, it's hard to picture football before the abolition of the maximum wage rule in January 1961. Brian, except for a few months before the injury that finished him, played his entire career for restricted rewards.

He was averaging forty goals a season for Middlesbrough but being paid the same wage as myself, an average goalkeeper. That was £17 a week, which wasn't even the permitted maximum. I think the top pay in the league was £20 a week, plus, if you were lucky, a taxable benefit of £750 for each five years spent with a club.

Yet those were wonderful, enjoyable days for us, setting the scene for our success later. Our clubmates were mostly in the snooker halls while we were out coaching schoolboys at Redcar or standing behind the goal at Darlington or anywhere else that we could find a game on a free afternoon. We told the truth to the headmaster at Redcar: 'We've no coaching qualifications.' He said, 'I don't care; I'll judge you on what you do.' The pay was £1 4 shillings each for an hour, which was good for those days, but the bonus was the pleasure of working with youngsters.

We ought to have enrolled for an FA coaching course, but we felt that Walter Winterbottom, the FA's director of coaching, as well as manager of the England team, had allowed himself to be surrounded by spouting theorists. We resented schoolmasters who posed as authorities on a game of which they had no professional experience.

The pair of us were obsessed with football. All our time went in training for it, playing it, watching it in the old northeast Wednesday League and arguing about it. For variation, we sometimes played each other at tennis, squash, badminton, table tennis or billiards. Brian always hated to lose.

I remember a winger complaining to the Middlesbrough training staff that Brian had knocked him off the ball before an open goal and scored himself. Brian's answer, when questioned about the incident, was undiluted Clough – 'Well, I'm better at it than he is.'

That was his outlook on almost everything: 'I can do it better. What's more, I'll prove it.' He seemed pushy, a know-all and arrogant – but never forget that arrogance is an asset in a footballer. Anyone could see how Brian might upset people, yet I liked him. He was clean-cut; there was nothing, then or now, treacherous in his nature and, unusually for someone so full of himself, he could stand a little ribbing.

'Why aren't you out dancing?' I asked when he was round my house every night. 'You're growing old too quickly, you ought to spread your wings.' But Brian at twenty was in love with football and cricket.

'What wouldn't I give to have opened the batting for England?' he used to sigh, a clear case of ambition exceeding talent. He might have fielded to Test standard, he was so quick, alert and sure-handed, but in all the pre-season cricket we played together, I never saw him look anything better than a reasonable club batsman.

Football, though, was something else and it is amazing that

England capped him only twice, especially when the death of Tommy Taylor in the Manchester United air crash of 1958 forced them to look everywhere for a centre-forward, even to the extent of recalling the Bolton veteran Nat Lofthouse. Week after week, I stood in Middlesbrough's goalmouth watching Brian make my predictions come true at the other end. Defensive systems were simpler in our playing days; teams didn't field two centre-backs and so centre-forwards were always in the ideal situation of one-against-one.

How Brian banged in the goals for us: thirty-eight in his first full season, followed by forty, forty-three, thirty-nine and thirty-four in the succeeding seasons. I believe he would have been curtailed only slightly by the modern tactic of a sweeper supporting the centre-half. You can either score goals or you can't. Brian was blessed with the scorer's knack and he would have stuck goals away in any company if the players around him supplied the chances.

All but one of his goals – and that when he was a virtual crock – were scored in the Second Division and the knockers always asked, 'Would he have succeeded in the First?' Of course he would have done. He would have succeeded with England, too. They said he lacked mobility but Brian was mobile where it mattered. He saved his energy for the penalty box; he lurked there always, awake to the faintest chance and applying the clinical finish.

His frustration over Middlesbrough's failure to win promotion led to clashes with teammates, who organised a round robin to remove him from the captaincy. Most clubs prefer a skipper in midfield where it is easier to communicate with all the team's departments, but I believe in choosing captains for leadership, irrespective of their position. Brian was a born leader. He had been head boy at Marton Grove secondary school at Middlesbrough and his fellow pupils have said, 'He stood out. He got respect from everyone, he almost demanded it.'

I wasn't surprised by the story of the day he started work as a fifteen-year-old messenger at ICI, when he was immediately given charge of a group of boys. I remember one of them recalling, 'It must have seemed automatic to the bosses because he had such a forceful nature. Some people might say he's arrogant but we just accepted him as someone who knew his own mind.' ICI promoted him later to a clerkship in the work study department, which meant clocking on at twelve minutes past seven every morning and provoked a typical grumble – 'Can you imagine a sillier time? Which genius thought that up?'

Brian, in my opinion, was the right appointment as captain of Middlesbrough because the team needed the spur of a dedicated winner, but it turned into another example of strong characters begetting strong reactions. Clough as skipper presented an opportunity to players who had been waiting to voice their personal dislike. I was pounding round the track one morning when Brian Phillips, the centre-half, said, 'We're not happy about your mate being skipper and we're doing something about it. We've got a round robin, but I know you won't sign it.'

'Dead right,' I told him. 'What's more, you're out of order. You can't win.' Nevertheless, eight or nine players signed the petition. Eric Thomas, the club chairman, called a meeting and asked them individually to explain their action. The players backed down and Brian continued to carry out the ball, but his departure had become inevitable. He was too hot to handle and I remember the chairman warning him, 'Don't finish as a martyr.'

Middlesbrough's manager Bob Dennison, although one of my favourite people, was too unambitious for Brian, and his staff were in the same easygoing mould. Harold Shepherdson, the England trainer, and coaches like Micky Fenton and Jimmy Gordon were nice men running a pleasant club that treated players decently while getting nowhere.

I signed for Port Vale for £750, my benefit money, on 12 June 1961 and was sunning myself in a deckchair at Scarborough when Middlesbrough decided to rid themselves of the rebellious Clough. Brian himself found me by the North Bay and broke the news. 'Sunderland have been on, wanting yes or no

before I go on holiday tomorrow, but I'd rather play for Cullis.'
Stan Cullis, the manager of Wolverhampton Wanderers, was
renowned for producing high-scoring teams whose use of
wingers, the long ball and continual attack had won the FA
Cup once and the League Championship twice in the previous
three seasons. No official approach had been made by Cullis
to Middlesbrough but we weren't concerned about the nice-
ties. We walked to the nearest phone box and I rang Wolves.
Unfortunately, Cullis was away and I had to speak to his chief
scout, George Noakes, who, oddly for his profession, had only
one eye and that eye was not focused on Brian Clough.

Noakes, either through lack of authority or lack of interest, declined to jump the gun. I hung up, wondering, 'What
next?' Then, as a gambling man, I saw how to profit from
the fact that Brian's impending transfer was known only to
ourselves and the managers and chairmen of Sunderland and
Middlesbrough, who wanted it kept quiet for the time being.
The bookies, already drawing up their promotion odds for the
coming season, knew nothing of it.

'I'll get a bet on if you think it won't leak out for a while,'
I told Brian.

'No one will find out from me; I'm off on a cruise tomorrow.'

I popped back into the call box and phoned a friend.
'What's the best price you can get against Sunderland for
promotion next season?'

'How much do you want to bet?'

'Eighteen quid,' which was just over a week's wages.

'I'll fish around,' he said.

Sunderland's manager Alan Brown was waiting at Southampton docks with the transfer forms when Brian sailed home again but, by then, I was sitting pretty. The news sent the odds tumbling to 7–2 against Sunderland but, through my inside information and a head start, I had been laid the fantastic price of 100–6. I could win £300 for my outlay of £18 and, until the very last match, it seemed that I had pulled off a coup by betting on Brian – but then Sunderland failed against lowly Swansea and missed promotion by a point.

Middlesbrough Football Club hugged themselves with delight at making £42,000 profit from unloading a supposed troublemaker to their closest Second Division rivals, but their priorities were completely wrong and the proof is that it took them another fourteen years to win promotion. Middlesbrough were the wrong club for Brian because they didn't know how to cope with a radical going crazy to burst into the First Division. He represented a guaranteed forty goals a season and Middlesbrough ought to have built a team round him.

The tragedy of Brian as a footballer, and I'm not thinking only of the premature end to his career, was the failure not only of his club, but also of his country, to capitalise on his extraordinary talent. England capped him only twice because Winterbottom and his amateur selectors wanted runners, forwards like Derek Kevan and Ray Pointer, who cover every blade of grass while scoring once in 1,000 miles.

CHAPTER 3

HANGING UP OUR BOOTS

Brian left Middlesbrough on 14 July 1961 and played one full season for Sunderland; his second season was interrupted by the worst winter that I've known in football. It began on Boxing Day 1962 and caused chaos for two months. The FA Cup final was put back for three weeks, hundreds of matches were postponed and the pools panel was created to guess the results of the unplayed games.

Brian Clough was among the first casualties of the snow and ice; he skidded on a freezing pitch at Roker Park on Boxing Day and wrecked his right knee colliding with Bury's goalkeeper, Chris Harker. The reports in next morning's newspaper highlighted Sunderland's first home defeat of the season before mentioning that their 24-goal centre-forward had been carried off. Johnny Watters, Sunderland's physiotherapist, was among the few men who realised immediately the seriousness of that Boxing Day injury. He said:

> Brian was about to kick the ball when the goalkeeper slid across his lower leg; I knew something bad had happened by the way Brian fell; indeed, it caused further damage to his knee.
>
> I found a complete tear of the cruciate and medial ligaments; injuries to the cruciate, which is a sort of St Andrew's cross, are inoperable or, I should say, there is no satisfactory operation.
>
> I treated Brian for a year. The important factor in orthopaedics is the contribution of the patient and Brian was first class; he cooperated to the hilt in running laps and in running up and down and back up again on the terraces.
>
> He came back to play for Sunderland, but he knew that he would never be the same.

Brian scored only one more league goal after the injury and Sunderland had to wait eighteen months for it; by then, they were back in the First Division. He played three games for them and scored the only First Division goal of his career against a Leeds United defence featuring England's centre-half Jackie Charlton.

The goal pleased him but his overall performance confirmed the gloomiest forecasts. 'My sharpness has gone,' he told me, refusing to fool himself. He had scored 251 league goals in 271 games and it was all over by the age of twenty-nine. Brian turned out in friendlies and fundraising fixtures afterwards – once with Sir Stanley Matthews at Burton – but his role was restricted to what professionals call 'a standing-around job'. He simply couldn't turn as in the old days, and it was a pitiful end for someone so proud of hardly ever being absent through injury or illness and who so often said to me, 'No one has ever enjoyed scoring goals more than I do.'

Barbara Clough seems to believe the injury drives her husband and that Brian perhaps hungers for the recognition denied him outside the north-east for his playing ability. He was often written off by Fleet Street as a mere Second Division hot-shot whose goals won no cups or medals and who failed to score in his two appearances for England.

I think the iron entered deeper into his soul because of the callous treatment he received from Sunderland once he was officially on the scrapheap. The club collected £40,000 compensation; Brian received £1,500 (doesn't that tell you a lot about football?) and they sacked him from the job of coaching their apprentices and part-timers. He had helped the juniors to the semi-final of the FA Youth Cup but that was no protection when the managers changed. George Hardwick, the former England captain who had appointed Brian, resigned; Ian McColl, a former manager of Scotland's national team, took over and sacked Brian at the end of the 1964–65 season.

Brian demanded an official reason for his dismissal but wasn't given one, although it seems to have been an economy cut. He was out of work for four months before Sunderland staged a benefit match for him on 28 October 1965. A total of 31,898 people came to see Brian for the last time in the red and white stripes and he scored both Sunderland's goals (although the second was a penalty that would have been disputed in anything but a friendly game).

While Brian had been at Sunderland my own career had been making the transition from playing to management. When I left Middlesbrough to join Port Vale I was in my mid-thirties and finished as a league goalkeeper, but Port Vale had nevertheless signed me. After a month, I said to the manager, Norman Low, 'You don't need me because you've got a lad called Ken Hancock who can play. All he needs is encouragement.' Hancock came into the side soon and was sold later to Tottenham Hotspur via Ipswich Town, while I moved out of the league in July 1962 and joined Burton Albion. I was at home one Sunday evening celebrating my daughter's birthday when Trevor Grantham, the chairman and an important man in my life, phoned to say, 'I've given Bill Townsend six weeks' notice as manager. Have you considered the job?'

'It's always been my intention to go into management.'

'Get an application in.'

I was appointed in 1963 but nearly sacked before getting a chance to establish myself. Non-league clubs like Burton live partly off the proceeds of runs in the FA Cup, so there was a crisis when my side made an early exit against lower-grade opposition. We were a Southern League club but lost 1–0 to Tamworth from the Birmingham League.

'That's not on,' said some directors, demanding a board meeting on the spot. I protested that it was neither the time nor place, so the meeting was postponed until the following morning at the chairman's house. Mr Grantham met me in the kitchen that Sunday, saying, 'They think they're going to cut your throat, but they're wrong!' I survived with his support and never looked back, and the experience of managing Burton was invaluable when I teamed up with Brian at Hartlepools in 1965.

CHAPTER 4

HARRY STORER

I said earlier that Brian and I are indebted for our creed as managers to a man called Harry Storer.

I hadn't been a professional footballer long before sensing that my vocation was for management. I began studying managers and their methods and saw several of them come and go during my nine years at Coventry, but Storer was the one who left a lasting impression and who opened my eyes. Micky Fenton, a trainer at Middlesbrough, once observed, 'It wasn't until Peter Taylor signed for us and started quoting Harry Storer that Brian Clough began to think deeply about football.'

I count myself lucky to have known Harry Storer, who was a member of that almost extinct breed of professional cricketer-footballers. Storer was an England international wing-half in the 1920s and a county opening batsman, whose partnership of 322 with Joe Bowden at Leyton has stood as Derbyshire's first wicket record for more than fifty years.

Everything said by Harry Storer on football management has stood the test of time. He boiled down the job to one sentence – 'It's easy to be a good manager; all you do is sign good players' – and then he would wink. He knew that was the hardest part of all.

Storer himself was a natural sportsman. He was blunt, yet also something of an orator and able to destroy almost anyone verbally. He was ruthless and often frightening, yet always fair. His strength was an enormous ability to want. He wanted to win, he wanted the truth. He wanted his own way which, in itself, was unusual in an era when directors lorded it over most clubs and kept their ex-professional footballer managers in subservience.

Even the England international team was selected – or, at least, recommended – by coal merchants and toffee-makers from the FA council, so it never occurred to many boardrooms that the manager, a mere employee, might dare to interfere with the directors' privilege of selecting the club's side. It was commonplace in the late '40s and early '50s to see managers shuffling outside in the corridors on Thursday nights while the board considered, and amended, the suggested team.

These directors never blamed themselves when the team lost. No, that was the manager's fault. Harry was probably the first to fight for the principle that the man risking the sack was entitled to the final say on selection. He wouldn't tolerate amateurs picking his team and I'll never forget his rebuke of one meddling director.

'What is your profession, sir?' asked Harry.

'I'm a brewer.'

'What would you say if I were to visit your brewery tomorrow and tell you how to improve the beer?'

'I'd say that you were damned impertinent.'

Harry pounced, 'And that's exactly what I'm telling you.'

I learned from Storer's attitude towards directors. He handled them with a self-assurance that sprang from being good at his job and winning promotion for three clubs: Coventry City, Birmingham City and Derby County. I saw how he dominated players; for instance, when he descended on a skulking forward and demanded before the whole dressing room: 'Show me where it is.' The player was dumbfounded.

'Where what is, boss?'

'Come back on the pitch this minute and show me,' Harry bellowed.

'I don't know what you mean,' said the player, now thoroughly alarmed. 'What do you want to see?'

'*The hole*,' he spoke with a terrifying roar. 'That hole you're hiding in every bloody match.'

Football managers were not national figures in those days, but Harry Storer was heard occasionally on radio sports programmes with much the same shock effect as Brian Clough today. He was outspoken, candid and spared nobody. He was scathing about coaches, saying, 'They're telling us we should copy the Continentals and have retreating defences. When an opponent has the ball, they say we should fall back until he makes a mistake – but they have no answer when I ask them, "Suppose he doesn't make a mistake?"' Coaches, a word that Harry almost spat out, had no answer, either, to his stock challenge. 'There are hundreds of coaches and miles of film showing exactly how Stanley Matthews used to beat a fullback. Yet where is the coach who has taught just one lad how to perform the same trick?'

Some professionals, particularly coaches, regarded him as abrasive and abusive and I once heard a trainer at Middlesbrough complaining of 'Storer's disgraceful manner', so I asked, 'But what about the content; wasn't it brilliant?'

Harry's message about being the boss, finding the best players and standing no nonsense was so simple that it went unheeded, but not by me. I was Storer's pupil. He taught me what to look for in a player and I disagreed only with his emphasis on defence and overemphasis on physical courage and bodily contact. Joe Mercer, when manager of Sheffield United, phoned Harry to protest after a bruising visit by Derby.

'I don't know why you bothered to bring a ball,' said Joe. 'Two of your players didn't need one. They kicked us, instead.'

'Which two?' snapped Harry, who had missed the match to go scouting. 'Give me their names.'

Joe, always the nice guy, demurred. 'Oh, no. I don't wish to get them into trouble.'

'Give me their names!'

Joe considered it. 'Only if you promise not to punish them.'

'I'll do nothing to *them*,' cried Harry. 'I'm going to crucify the other nine!'

Harry admired skilful footballers provided they also shaped like prospective VCs. I can still hear him musing, 'Yes, I agree that lad can play – but can he play when some big, angry bloke is trying to stop him?' He scouted for Everton as an old man when he was out of management and they still remember receiving from him the shortest possible report on a player. It was one word in capitals across the reporting form: COWARD.

I was fascinated by Storer and would go out of my way after leaving Coventry to consult the oracle, often in just a few minutes of conversation on railway platforms as our teams waited for Saturday night trains – but I disliked his prejudice against cowards and told him so. I prefer to sign brave footballers but have always seen plenty of scope for those who are less foolhardy; indeed, the word coward is one that I never apply to players. Harry remained adamant, though, that a footballer was useless if he shrank from challenges and the risk of injury. He said, 'There's never been a player who enjoyed being kicked but some endure it better than others. They are my kind of player.'

I hope Harry Storer doesn't sound like a bayonet drill instructor; there was more to him than that, including a soft, human side under the peppery manner. He was also a rarity for the times in being a reasonably educated man in a business much given to such howlers as talking of 'harmonium in the dressing room' and instructing a player, 'Son, when you veer, try to veer straight.' Not all the illiterates were on the pitch, either. I remember a disciplinary committee where a First Division chairman, who was also a member of the league's management committee, told the players brought before him, 'I can promise you boys a most pathetic hearing.'

Storer died in the summer of 1967 shortly after Brian Clough and I joined Derby County, a step from which he tried to dissuade us. He said, 'Make your own decision but, if you're advised by me, you'll turn it down because the composition of the board is a scandal' – adding, in true Storer style, 'and I've told the directors so as well.' I took some whisky to his house and broke the news that, despite our respect for his opinion, we were going to the Baseball Ground. I'm sad that he never saw the success which we brought to Derby County, but hardly a day goes by without Brian or I asking ourselves, 'Now what would Harry have done here?'

CHAPTER 5

HARTLEPOOLS – BOTTOM RUNG OF THE LADDER

The morning after Brian's testimonial match at Sunderland, as agreed between us at York, we began work together at Hartlepools. Brian captured the following day's sports headlines with his answer to a question about how it felt to be the league's youngest manager:

'Age does not count. It's what you know about football that matters. I know I am better than the 500 or so managers who have been sacked since the war. If they had known anything about the game, they wouldn't have lost their jobs.'

Before anyone could compose a suitably tart retort, we won our first three matches – against Bradford City and Crewe Alexandra in the league and against Workington in the FA Cup.

Brian kept firing away with pungent quotes in those early

weeks; he was controversial, yet sensible, and I remember a statement that remains the foundation of his beliefs about management: 'In this business you've got to be a dictator, or you haven't a chance.' Another time he summed up our task in a paragraph: 'There's only one way out for a small club – good results and then more good results. How hard it is to get them few people will ever know.'

Believe me, it was doubly hard at Hartlepools, football's rock bottom. Someone told me just after our arrival that the club had been losing since the First World War when a Zeppelin bombed the ground and the directors unsuccessfully sued the Kaiser.

Hartlepools had been compelled to beg for re-election in six of the seven seasons before signing us, and any year in which they hadn't conceded 100 goals was regarded as a comparative golden age. The players, except for a goalkeeper and a forward who came with me from Burton Albion, were mostly free transfers and several of them had personal problems with drink, debt or abandoned wives. We had to discipline some and sack others; one we had to bail out after he had been arrested at the ground for non-payment of maintenance to his wife.

Jeyes Fluid was our biggest signing in that first season; we spent more on disinfectant than on players. The Victoria Ground was a mess, but we made sure it was a clean mess. Once, rummaging around the stand rafters, I came across a pile of poultry feathers and was greatly puzzled until learning that Fred Westgarth, one of our many predecessors as manager of Hartlepools, kept bantam chickens there, removing them only on match days. Brian and I painted that stand. We unblocked the drains, cut the grass, unloaded corrugated iron to shelter the terraces and, after every rainy night, emptied the buckets.

Hartlepools United leaked all over. The roof let water into the dressing rooms, into the boardroom (which was a hut under the stand) and into Brian's office, where the drips fell on our heads as we used the phone. Shortage of money cramped us continually. We couldn't do anything about the notorious dressing room where the copper cistern projected across the visiting team's bath in such a way that anyone standing up carelessly could be knocked senseless. We couldn't afford a new ball for every match as the regulations required; instead, we washed and waxed the old ones so expertly that they sometimes lasted for a month if the referees were sympathetic enough not to scrutinise too closely. Tracksuits? An unimagined luxury. Why, after February, we couldn't even afford new boots for the players; there was no sense, with only a couple of months left, in buying boots for lads whom we wouldn't be keeping for next season. Our players knew their fate without needing to wait for the official retained list in April; they knew by their footwear.

No one owned personal kit, so training began with a general rummage through a pile of motley gear on the dressing room table. 'Help yourself, lads. First come, first served,' I'd tell them, while knowing it was unlikely that we had enough socks to go round. It was common in our practice matches to see professionals playing in street socks.

Once, probably in debt to the coach firm and unable to raise enough for train fares, we drove the team in three cars to a league match at Barnsley. Total outlay: twenty gallons of petrol, fish and chips for fourteen and, surprisingly, win bonuses for eleven.

We finished seventh from the bottom after that first season, an almost stratospheric placing for a team over-staffed with deadbeats and renegades whom we dared not leave alone for a moment; I'm not thinking of capers off the field but of their incapacity to absorb instructions on it. The poorer the footballer, the more attention he needs. Basic drills at throw-ins, corners and free kicks must be hammered into their thick heads and, even then, are often forgotten in the stress of a match.

The bottom half of the Fourth Division is the managerial end of the world; Brian and I experienced all the difficulties – incompetent players, public apathy, poverty and a ramshackle ground. Our biggest problem, though, was only five feet tall. He was the chairman! Ernest Ord grew rich in the war. He was in clothing and trading checks and was reputed to be a millionaire; he drove a Rolls with his face just above the level of the steering wheel. I disliked him from the start.

'Your first job is to avoid an application for re-election. If we have to ask again, the league will probably throw us out,' he warned when appointing us. Brian's answer was to wake up the town by arousing press interest and reminding everyone that Hartlepools United were alive and kicking under new, youthful management.

We arranged some stunt training on the beach in our second week at the club. Pictures appeared in national newspapers; we were delighted, but Mr Ord was displeased. 'You'll have to cut it out,' he ordered. 'You're getting too much publicity.' We were thunderstruck. The club seemed to be a toy for him. No doubt he had the best interests of Hartlepools at heart but he had a strange way of showing it, and I always had the impression that he only wanted enough success to keep in the league with himself in control. He struck me as one of those little men who need power to compensate for their lack of inches and I felt he used football as a way to throw his weight about.

I can see him now, those tiny eyes glaring and stubby legs swinging as he perched on the edge of the boardroom table ordering inquisitions.

'Fetch Simpkins in,' he might command. Or Green

or Parry or any other name which happened to pop into his head.

'Where were you last night?'

'Went to the pictures, sir. Then went home.'

'Don't lie to me. I know you players and I want the truth.'

If Brian and I have known more than our share of conflict with directors over the years, then the seeds of trouble were sown at Hartlepools. The chairman's behaviour was inexcusable, a gross interference with a manager's duties, yet we had to swallow it. We were starting our careers and wanted to be successful; if we walked out, there might not be another opening. Brian wanted to leave a dozen times; he packed his bags, but I persuaded him to stay. I apologised to the unfortunate players summoned for browbeating, explaining, 'It's a dreadful situation but if you don't come there'll be a head-on collision between the manager and the chairman.'

Each afternoon, a few minutes before five, the phone rang in Brian's office but no one was on the line when he picked it up; he suspected it was the chairman checking up on whether we were working a full day.

'You'll never beat that fellow,' people in the town told us, because they knew that Ernest Ord held the club in his grip through guaranteeing its debts; sometimes players could not be paid until Friday afternoon because the bank refused to release the wages without Ord's authorisation. He was also owed £7,000 by the club, a millstone for a little outfit like Hartlepools.

Yet we saw a glimmer of hope in the moral courage of another director, Councillor John Curry. We asked him to back us against the chairman; we knew that, given the right support, our complaints about interference could topple Mr Ord. There was no gain in a coup for Councillor Curry, but he agreed to side with us and so the apparently impossible was achieved. Mr Ord resigned only a year after our arrival.

Brian was in his element afterwards; every day brought a fresh idea or a new headline. He took lessons for a public service vehicle licence so that he could qualify to drive the team's bus. He worked for two months without wages, living on his savings up to Christmas 1966. His sacrifice of £40 a week (which I, a believer in charity beginning at home, didn't copy) stirred the town's imagination and brought sponsors forward. Cameron's brewery announced that they would pay the wages of one player; the shipyards and working men's clubs rattled with collecting boxes, even old-age pensioners sent us 10 shillings a week.

Brian toured the town, lecturing every night for a fortnight in February 1967, in a successful attempt to raise £7,000 to pay off our ex-chairman and banish the spectre of liquidation. People responded to his youth and enthusiasm. I remember a letter from a lodge of the Royal Antediluvian Order of

Buffaloes promising £50 a time from a series of monthly concerts. A typical evening included raffles, bingo and a cabaret at the Rovers Quoits Club with Brian on the microphone drumming up donations.

He was never out of the north-east news and even made the political pages by canvassing for the Conservative Councillor Curry in the borough elections. Brian, a staunch socialist who had been offered the Labour parliamentary candidature at Richmond (Yorks) a couple of years earlier, had his explanation ready: 'I am bound to support this man for what I've seen him do for the club and the town in recent months.' No one foresaw that Mr Curry, by then chairman of Hartlepools, was only a few weeks away from picking up his phone one Saturday night to hear Brian say, 'Sorry, but we're resigning.'

Len Shackleton had again played fairy godfather to us by phoning Derby County after the sacking of manager Tim Ward. A shortlist had been drawn up by Sam Longson, Derby's chairman, and I believe the names were Tommy Cummings, Billy Bingham and Alan Ashman. We had never crossed Derby's mind until Shackleton told them, 'I've got two young blokes who are just right for your job.' His fame as a player was so great that we promptly shot to the top of Longson's list, one of the breaks that everyone needs in life.

Brian met Longson at Scotch Corner on the A1, then the two of us met the Derby directors and, finally, we took our families to the Royal Hotel at Scarborough and thrashed out our future through three days of incessant rain. I wanted to go, but Brian didn't. He was happy in the north-east; we had finished our second season only eighth from top because of players giving us more effort than we had expected. He thought we were assembling a decent side and should see things through.

We weren't on contract at Hartlepools but, out of courtesy, had advised the board of Derby's interest. Someone told the secret to a businessman and keen supporter, who called at my house and offered me £1,000 in notes to stay. I had never seen so much money, yet I still, as I've done all these years, argued a case calculated to change Brian's mind. I said, 'Look, we took Hartlepools only as a stepping stone to something better and now that's come along. Derby County have tradition; they can become a good club again. You know yourself that it's been a hard slog at Hartlepools and, personally, I've had a bellyful of it. I know we can never pick the perfect time to go but I think this is the right move for us.'

My strength lay in buying but there had been only £7,500 to spend at Hartlepools, of which £4,000 had to go on one man, a terrifyingly tough centre-half from Mansfield Town called Johnny Gill. The attraction of Derby was a promise of £70,000 for new players; the figure was mentioned during our interview with the Derby board, which, as always with us, was a two-way affair. We interviewed them, too; not merely about salaries and working conditions but about the size of their ambitions for the club. The boldness of our approach surprised them and they were certainly startled when Brian reinforced our arguments for a contract by telling Sam Longson, 'Mr Chairman, you've got seven directors here and, inside a month, one of them will want to get rid of us.'

How prophetic were those words, although there were years of triumph and huge signings between that summer of 1967 and the inevitable crisis.

CHAPTER 6

BUILDING A TEAM
AT DERBY

I started my real work for Derby County amid a crowd of ordinary spectators standing behind the goal at a Third Division match. Advertising doesn't pay in the scouting business, so neither club knew I was there, nor could any of the fans around me have guessed that I had no interest in the result of the match but only in the performance of the visiting team's eighteen-year-old centre-half.

It was a summer evening in Devon, the first Saturday of the 1967–68 season with only one night match on the fixture list: Torquay United *v.* Tranmere Rovers, which my mind translated into Jim Fryatt *v.* Roy McFarland. I had seen McFarland playing against us at Hartlepools and recognised him immediately as an uncut diamond; he was almost top of my reasons for being so keen to join Derby and spend their £70,000.

Fryatt was a big centre-forward of the type always tagged as 'much travelled', meaning that he had played for nine different league clubs to my knowledge. He was clever in the air, no mug on the floor by Third Division standards and is still the holder of the fastest goal record – four seconds from the kick-off for Bradford against Tranmere in 1965, although this timing by the referee is regarded with widespread scepticism. The duel between them put me on the rack because Fryatt gave young McFarland a roasting. I came to understand the difference between assessing a player when the transfer is a dream and looking at the same man when the cash is in your hand and the deal a reality.

I had never discussed McFarland with anyone, not even with Brian Clough. Strange as it may sound, we never talk at length about possible signings; instead, he waits for me to tell him, 'I've seen one,' then he pounces.

My first sight of McFarland gave me the same thrill as my first sight of Brian. I knew that the moment we had money to spend my target would be Tranmere's centre-half, but I needed to check him out again and, for that purpose, there could hardly have been a sterner examiner than Fryatt. Yet the kid never lost composure and I noted again his cultured left foot and his ruthlessness. I told Brian, 'It's what I thought. We're in.'

Tranmere were due to play their first home game on the

following Friday, so we phoned their manager Dave Russell for an appointment a couple of hours before the kick-off. 'I'll be glad to see you, my lads,' he said, 'but who are you interested in?' I lied, and not very convincingly as it turned out, 'Those two lads, the Kings, who are in your side.'

Russell had been around too long to fall for that, and when we arrived he said to us, 'Don't beat around the bush. If we're going to do business, you'll have to mark my card. I think it's my young centre-half, not the Kings, who has brought you up here and I can tell you he's available for the right price. See me after the game.'

The directors' box overflowed with managers and scouts, so the only spare seat for me was in the press box alongside Paddy Ryan, who scouted for West Bromwich Albion. 'Who are you after, then?' he asked near the finish; annoyed at being considered a novice whose brains were easy to pick, I nodded towards the opposing centre-forward, John Sainty of Reading, saying, 'Not bad, that number nine.' Then I left and walked from Prenton Park (uniquely, Tranmere's headquarters are outside the ground) and joined Brian in the official tea room before slipping upstairs to the manager's office.

Dave Russell was not impressed by our opening bid of £9,000, but thawed slowly as we inched towards £20,000. We called a halt at that point and asked to use the phone, explaining, 'This is getting so high that we'll need sanction from the chairman.' An eavesdropper, had there been one, would have heard Brian earnestly seeking permission to pay a fee that might go as high as £24,000, but there was no Sam Longson at the other end. Brian was talking down a line that rang unanswered in his own office, a charade to stop Tranmere from discovering that we could spend more than £40,000 and were answerable only to ourselves.

It was 1 a.m. when we shook hands with Dave Russell on £24,000 and followed his car under the Mersey tunnel towards the little terraced house where Roy McFarland lived in Liverpool with his parents. He wasn't in. We tried a club that he sometimes visited after matches. He wasn't there either. Brian said to Dave, 'Lead us back to his house and we'll wait there if his mum and dad will stand for it.' Roy, by then, was back home and already in bed. He came down in his pyjamas. We had arranged the chairs so that he had to sit between us. Dave Russell introduced us and delivered the customary speech: 'These gentlemen are from Derby County and I've agreed a fee with them. If you want to go, Roy – and, of course, you don't have to – you can become a Derby player.' Poor Roy was taken aback. He was so young, he wasn't a publicised player, he wasn't in demand and few people outside Birkenhead had heard of him. He looked for some advice from his manager but Dave Russell, after a long day, had gone home.

Our sales talk didn't work with Roy, a safety-first type who wanted time to mull it over. He was a Liverpool lad, an Anfield fan and, I suppose, hoped always that Bill Shankly would send for him one day. Going to somewhere like Derby had never occurred to him. The conversation faltered, then his dad chimed in and began talking about a goal scored by Brian at Liverpool. It was the break we needed; we dropped Roy and talked football to his father, winning him over. In the end, and I'll never forget it because McFarland was the best signing of my career, he turned to his son, saying, 'Roy, if you're advised by me you'll sign for these gentlemen now, not tomorrow.' And he did.

Dawn was breaking over the Potteries when we stopped at a transport cafe on the road home. I reminded Brian over a mug of tea, 'You'd better mark the board's card before they meet him. With that baby face, they might think we've squandered their money on a schoolboy.'

A few hours later I believe that Shankly reached for a phone and blasted Dave Russell for not warning him of our swoop, but Liverpool themselves had been complacent. Big Ron Yeats was the unshakeable centre-half in a winning Anfield team, so the club view on McFarland seemed to be, 'He's always just round the corner should we need him.' Liverpool's annoyance over our raid was more understandable than the envy of clubs who claimed, 'You only just pipped us, you know.' They sickened me. We pipped nobody for McFarland; a future England star had been available to anyone prepared to back their judgement. He won twenty-eight international caps and at his peak, before a series of injuries, was the finest footballing centre-half in Europe. The people of Derby, a town much given to memories when we arrived, should number McFarland among their greatest players.

Derby County had been a brilliant team as the war ended, and won the FA Cup handsomely with four goals against Charlton Athletic in the first post-war final, but over the next twenty years were notable mainly for sliding from the First Division to the Third in three appalling seasons. Harry Storer lifted them back to the Second Division and they had remained stuck there for a decade until we arrived. Brian was scornful of Derby. 'Full of nostalgia,' he would snort to me. 'There's Raich Carter, Billy Steel and Peter Doherty round every corner.' Brian is identified closely with Derby now and kept his home there even while managing Leeds United, Brighton and Forest, but the truth is that he never wanted to work in the Midlands.

Derby meant nothing to him then, his north-eastern ambitions extended no further than managing Sunderland or Newcastle United and he often accused me, 'You've only come here because it's next door to your home town.' That wasn't my reason at all. I wanted to join Derby County because I am a traditionalist; I believe that clubs which have been great once can be great again. Derby was a traditional football town and I knew the right team would fill the Baseball Ground.

There are some superstitious folk in Derby. Only last season a medium exorcised the ghost of a man murdered a century earlier at the Baseball Ground, as though a phantom was the cause of their relegation plight. Our arrival in Derby provided excuses to trot out the ancient tale that the ground, once a Romany encampment, had been cursed by the evicted gypsies who swore the team would never win a trophy. The weakness in the curse story was the 1946 triumph in the FA Cup. The reasons for Derby's problems, as we soon discovered, were anything but supernatural. On average gates of only 13,000, they tried to support four professional teams from a playing staff that was too large, somewhat undisciplined and of only moderate ability. The training ground was a horror for a club with pretensions; it was one pitch off the ring road with an old railway carriage for dressing rooms.

The Derby symbol is a ram (incidentally, Brian's astrological sign) and we went in like charging rams. Our cry was, 'Observe, expose, replace'; many of those Derby players feared our opinion of them and so did some members of the non-playing staff. Quite a number left quietly of their own accord, others were sacked. I think the casualties at the end of our first season totalled sixteen players, four groundsmen, some caterers, a couple of clerks and a tea lady who laughed after a bad defeat.

The board, as one man, had said, 'Get on with it,' and we did, despite the defeatism of people like a chain-smoker in the office who kept saying, 'I've seen it all before here, new brooms coming in and sorting everyone out.' I told him, 'What you mean is that managers come and go but secretarial staff go on for ever. Just be careful this time that the reverse doesn't happen.'

Brian, as well as shaking up the club, was busy rousing the town. It was the Hartlepools campaign again. He talked to anyone, journalist or organisation, willing to listen. He addressed the Rotary Club and the Round Table. He sold tickets, he stoked the club's boilers and got Derby County into the newspapers by doing so.

The wage structure was revised to give the players more incentives. In a few sentences, he destroyed the club's illusion that their youth scheme guaranteed future success. He said, 'It's no use telling supporters they must wait another three seasons to win something. Youth schemes are only one ingredient in the cake. We have to spend more.' That's where I came in, by finding Roy McFarland, who, although top of my list, was actually our second signing for Derby because Brian had spent £21,000 on a young forward who had been coached by him at Sunderland.

Brian professes to be the worst judge in football, but this transfer stood the test of time; the signing was John O'Hare, who was still playing in the First Division for us at Forest last season. O'Hare was the original target man, going bravely where others feared to tread and accepting the kicks and punches that are the lot of the back-to-goal striker. O'Hare with pace would have been a world-class footballer; without it, his close control, accuracy in passing and exemplary character kept him valuable to our teams for thirteen seasons.

Another signing to stand the test of time cost only £7,000 from Hartlepools; he was a boy we first saw riding up on a bike for a public trial. We never turned away any aspirant at Hartlepools, and our early Sundays there were devoted to staging matches in which batches of youngsters were slung on for half an hour. We never said, 'Don't call us, we'll call you,' but the atmosphere was not unlike auditions for a chorus line. I had seen about 150 no-hopers before my eye was caught by a tiny outside-right on the far side of the field. He was not particularly fast but he plonked the ball exactly where he wanted it and, rare among schoolboys, raised his head to size up the options.

'Close the gates,' I said to Brian. 'We want that nipper's signature.' It turned out more difficult than we expected because fourteen-year-old John McGovern was a pupil at a rugby-playing grammar school under a headmaster with a low opinion of soccer as a career, particularly at a Fourth Division club. The head relented in the end and it was a happy day when we signed McGovern as our first apprentice professional. We kept our promise to go back for him and he has been with us ever since, never giving less than full value.

I was lucky over another boy from the north-east – always a rich hunting ground – when watching two representative matches one Saturday. My morning prospect was a waste of time and the afternoon mission seemed equally fruitless until my attention was attracted by a short-haired, clean-cut wing-half.

'Don't know him,' said Barry Cornforth, our regional scout, 'but it's easy to find out.' Some thirty scouts were in the stand, sitting together as they always do. 'No inquiries here,' I warned. 'Walk out with me instead, and keep a straight face no matter what I say' – and then I blasted him, loudly enough to be overheard, for dragging me all the way from Derby to watch kids with no chance of developing into top-class professionals. Out of earshot, I said, 'I'll be home by eight, Barry. Ring me then with the lad's pedigree but be careful where you ask for it.' Sure enough, the phone rang almost as I walked through the door: 'His name's John Robson, aged seventeen, not tied to anyone but going to Newcastle United next week for a trial. He plays for a youth club at Birtley in County Durham.'

It's forbidden to sign players on Sunday but there is nothing in the regulations prohibiting a club from using the Sabbath to arrange a transfer. So at eleven on Sunday morning, not twenty-four hours after first setting eyes on John Robson, we were in the front room of his home – Brian and I, John and his parents, his sisters and brothers and the secretary of his youth club. We sent them a donation, we had John in our first team at eighteen and sold him later, complete with a League Championship medal, to Aston Villa as a £90,000 right-back. It was heartbreaking that multiple sclerosis put a premature, crippling end to his career.

By October 1967 we had Roy McFarland, John Robson, John O'Hare, Alan Hinton and already there – one of the few worthwhile legacies at Derby – striker Kevin Hector, who went on to win a couple of England caps. Those players became the nucleus of our promotion and championship sides, but teams take time to build; in that first season Chairman Longson was restless or trying to gee us up. We had been at Derby only three months when he summoned us before himself and vice-chairman Sydney Bradley, saying, 'I'm not happy with the way you two are operating.' He looked stern. We were flabbergasted and asked for a specific complaint but he didn't make one. I said, 'We haven't been here five minutes and you're unhappy already. I'm telling you we're absolutely on the right road.'

The final table didn't bear out those bold words, for we finished fifth from bottom of the Second Division in that 1967–68 season, yet we were full of hope. We knew a winning team was taking shape and that all we needed was a daring swoop for an overweight old fellow with a twice-broken leg. His name was Dave Mackay.

CHAPTER 7

PROMOTION AND CONSOLIDATION

Dave Mackay played as though bagpipes skirled in his ears, and with a fearlessness unsapped even by successive fractures. We wanted such an indomitable character. We also wanted Mackay because he spelled 'big time'. We were a run-down, overdrawn Second Division club and he was a star from Spurs and Scotland, someone able to jingle a chestful of medals. Most of all, we wanted him as the old head to captain a young team, but Spurs told us, 'You've no chance. He's going home to Edinburgh as manager of Hearts.'

However, one of Brian's outstanding qualities, along with decisiveness, is persistence. He jumped into his car at six o'clock one morning and drove to Tottenham on the strength of a tip that Mackay's move to Hearts was 'only 99 per cent certain'. Who else would chase such a slim chance? Brian told me later that Bill Nicholson, manager of Spurs and busy with the pre-season training, kept him waiting in a corridor for an hour before warning him, 'I think you're wasting your time. Dave's future is settled.' Nicholson then left for the training ground at Cheshunt, while Brian, determined not to go home without speaking to Mackay, filled in time by driving to the Oval and watching Surrey *v.* Yorkshire. The cricket ended in a lunchtime collapse, though, and so he was back at Tottenham an hour before the Spurs players returned.

Mackay was allowed to walk out on the pitch with Brian and talk business, and I came into the transaction the next day when Mackay turned up at Derby with his accountant and a solicitor. 'He's not easy, this one,' said Brian. 'You'd better talk to him in my office. Take the phone off the hook and I'll lock the door on you.'

Dave had played wing-half, and very occasionally inside-forward, all his life but we visualised him in a different position. I explained, 'We want you at the back, playing off the centre-half.'

He laughed, 'Look, I've had it. I'm a stone overweight, I'm nearly thirty-four, older than the manager here. And I can't run any more.'

I said, 'Plenty of games you won't need to run, you won't even break sweat and all that you'll need is your loaf and your tongue. We've got youngsters to run for you. They need a captain with your experience, someone who'll say, "Hold it. Stay. I'll have it." Our lads will respond to you.'

He laughed again, still unconvinced, 'With anyone else, it would work. But I'm finished.'

I replied, 'Let Brian and myself be the judges of that.' Then, as always with transfers, the talk turned to wages.

Dave wasn't a haggler. He asked for terms which were high but not unreasonable when bearing in mind that Spurs required only a nominal £5,000 fee. Brian figured that Mackay cost us £22,000, which was £5,000 to Spurs and the rest spread over a contract which made him the league's biggest earner for a season. He was on £250 a week, plus promotion bonuses that raised his total pay to £16,000 a year, more than was earned by such First Division stars as Bobby Moore, Denis Law and George Best. Ten years of inflation later, there are still First Division footballers earning no more than Dave Mackay made with us in the Second Division, but Brian and I never stint on fees or wages once sure of getting value for money.

Mackay was worth every penny but we also rewarded him with something that money can't buy. We gave him, as he is the first to agree, the best two years of a career that he imagined was sinking into the twilight. He led us straight into the First Division and he was elected by the Football Writers' Association as Footballer of the Year for 1968–69, jointly with

Manchester City right-back Tony Book. It was the first case of a dead-heat in the ballot.

Every game he played for us confirmed our theory of management: assemble good players, handle them properly and extract their best. Handling Dave was never a problem; he radiated confidence without being big-headed and convinced the team that they were too good for the Second Division. His big-time manner was never seen to better effect than after a shocking foul in our first season after promotion. A Mackay foul was always painful; he went straight through opponents, and this time – before the days of red and yellow cards – the referee intended to send him off. The lads told me afterwards how Dave treated the suggestion with disdain, saying, 'Send me off? Don't you know who I am? I'm Dave Mackay, captain of Derby County, and I won't allow you to send me off – but you may take my name, if you like.' And that's what the bewildered referee did.

A piece was missing from the jigsaw even after the signing of Mackay, and it cost us £63,000 to complete the pattern. The money went on a Scot from Sheffield United, a tiny bundle of trouble called Willie Carlin. We swooped for him after our fourth game of Mackay's first season, a 2–0 defeat at Huddersfield Town which left us looking like a probable relegation team, for we had taken only two points from a possible eight.

Carlin's arrival changed that overnight; we lost only one of our next twenty-two matches and won the Second Division by seven points. He was a wing-half, only 5ft 4in. tall, quick-thinking, nippy and no stranger to the disciplinary commission. Brian didn't mince words with him at the signing: 'Eighteen bookings and three sendings-off won't do for us, Willie, because we can't afford players who get suspended. I'm not asking you to foul and I'm not asking you to argue with referees, but I am telling you to behave yourself.'

The fee for Carlin indicated that our days of bargain buys were ending. We had picked up some snips for Derby, though – only £5,000 for Mackay, £7,000 to Rochdale for our old Hartlepools goalkeeper Les Green, £20,000 for seventeen-year-old goalkeeper Graham Moseley of Blackburn Rovers, £20,000 for the former England centre-forward Frank Wignall of Wolves and only £2,500 to Burton Albion for striker Richie Barker (who was the assistant manager of the Wolves team who played against Forest in the 1980 League Cup final).

Derby launched itself on a communal spree when we brought First Division football back to the Baseball Ground after a gap of sixteen years. Sydney Bradley, then chairman, proclaimed, 'Brian and Peter built an ocean liner out of a shipwreck,' but we knew the vessel needed expensive additions to the crew.

'All we have to do is to increase our skill; it's skill that counts,' said Brian. 'We'll never win anything without it.' Skill had attracted us to a Nottingham Forest winger who had been discarded by England and was being barracked by Forest supporters, who branded him a coward. Alan Hinton was one of our earliest and best acquisitions for Derby, but a Forest committee man was heard to crow on the night we signed him, 'We've done them two good and proper; we've got £29,000 for Hinton.' Only £29,000 for the best cross-er with both feet I've ever seen, a player with fair pace and superb control? We weren't the losers in that transfer.

The crowd moaned at Hinton because he wasn't a lionheart but, over the years, we found that Alan had his own brand of courage. He never hid from criticism or problems and with-stood dreadful blows in his private life, particularly the death of a son. Hinton, who made as many goals for Derby as John Robertson has done for Forest, was an after-midnight sign-ing. I walked round the cinder track at two in the morning with him trying to agree terms. He wanted more money or a longer contract and I was selling him the opportunity for a fresh start, saying, 'You're destined to play for us. Don't miss the chance.'

Forest also sold us our first six-figure signing, a classy Welsh international called Terry Hennessey, who cost £110,000. We saw him as the eventual replacement for Mackay because, although Terry could perform creditably in midfield, he was an unflappable sweeper. I can still picture his bald head rising above our besieged defence in his greatest game, when we drew 0–0 in Lisbon against Benfica in the 1972–73 European Cup. Unfortunately, a nasty ankle injury in a pre-season match at Port Vale curtailed Hennessey's career. He also suffered from cartilage damage and recovered only after a fashion from two operations, so he was never as successful as we had hoped.

We finished fourth from top of the First Division in 1969–70, which was excellent for a newly promoted team; but we knew they were short of pace and so I acted on a tip from the club secretary Stuart Webb who pushed the claims of a young Scot at his former club, Preston North End. 'If it's pace you're after, then Archie Gemmill's the one,' said Webb. I went to watch Gemmill and saw that the secretary was right. Archie was quick, fiery and competitive, and we agreed to buy him for £64,000.

Preston's manager was Alan Ball, father of England's Alan Ball. He agreed a fee with us but seemed as if he didn't want the deal to go through. 'He's not the player you think he is,' he called to me as we set off for Gemmill's house, where trouble awaited us because Archie's wife was anti-Clough. She had taken a dislike to Brian's TV appearances and he was trying to win her round when the next-door neighbour – Ken

Knighton, later the manager of Sunderland – knocked with news of Archie's parents phoning from Scotland. Archie, whose house wasn't on the phone, trotted off while Brian and I exchanged disbelieving looks. 'Probably Harry Catterick ringing from Everton,' I said, learning later that this guess hit the bull's-eye. Brian nodded, 'I'll have to stay here for the night, or we'll miss out.' He slept in the spare room, awoke with his charm on full beam and signed Archie over the cornflakes; so ended a 24-hour working day that showed why our recent pay rises were merited. Brian, when teased about his new salary of £15,000 being double that of the Archbishop of Canterbury, had an answer ready: 'I can only say that the Derby County ground is full, but the churches are empty.'

Our pounce on Gemmill had similarities to the signing of Roy McFarland, for the public were asking, 'Archie who?' while managers were gnashing their teeth and claiming, 'You just pipped us.' Gemmill joined Preston as an outside-left from St Mirren and had won a Scottish Under-23 cap without progressing to full international honours; that changed under us, for he enjoyed seven years in Scotland's senior team and played in the Argentina World Cup of 1978.

Archie was a strange mixture. A hard man, yet he would blush at a compliment. A tiger on the pitch and a lamb off it. A loyal friend yet a born moaner nicknamed 'the nark'. He was a perfectionist, striving always for a flawless performance, so he was irritated by my insistence, 'You can't deliver the ball.' It was largely true; I didn't say it just to get a rise out of him. Passing was the only weakness in his game, but how he worked to improve it.

Crowds at the Baseball Ground averaged only 13,000 before our arrival, but First Division football filled it. We needed a new stand and twice as many seats, at least. We wanted 12,000 seats sold to season-ticket fans; with that money in our hands before a ball was kicked, we could finance spectacular transfers. We knew the demand was enormous because people were ordering seats while the Ley Stand was still on the drawing board. A man walked into my office, riffled a roll of fivers and asked for half a dozen season tickets two years hence. It's interesting to note the cheapness of football at the start of the '70s. The best seats at Derby cost only £12.50 for a whole season, and match admission to the terraces was only 25p.

Transfer fees were comparatively low, too. When we joined Derby the record between league clubs was only £110,000 – the fee paid by Everton to Blackpool for young Alan Ball after the 1966 World Cup. We set a new record twice in the next five years.

The first was £175,000 for Colin Todd of Sunderland in 1971. Brian did the deal off his own bat and sent a cheeky cable to chairman Sam Longson, who was on holiday in the West Indies, saying, 'We're running short of money. Get back quick.' Derby made only two signings in which I played no part. Todd was one, the other was John O'Hare, and both of them had been coached by Brian at Sunderland. Todd's natural ability was so impressive that sportswriters dubbed him 'the almighty Todd'. He was a hard, clean tackler, he was powerful and quick, his character was exemplary and Brian often kidded him, 'Toddy, you must lie, cheat or steal in private, because you're just too good to be true.'

Todd, though, had a failing – he lacked ambition. Kevin Keegan summed him up when remarking that Colin would rather play darts in a pub than win an England cap. This flaw showed in his football by cramping his vision; he would play short stuff instead of delivering the killer ball. We used Todd at right-back and we picked him in midfield, but his best position was sweeper because of his ability to retrieve, collect and win balls around the box without committing fouls. Many people imagined Colin Todd as a midfield player, but Brian and I knew that his creative instinct was limited. Sweeper was Colin's spot and his best years were alongside Roy McFarland.

Our second record signing was David Nish from Leicester City in 1972. The fee of £225,000, the highest in league history up to that time, was particularly staggering because Nish was a full-back and they were always valued lower than forwards. The deal was also criticised for flying in the face of the tradition that a defender's first duty is to win the ball. Nish was anything but intimidating in the tackle, but I didn't care.

My views on full-backs had been transformed by watching a friendly at Sheffield Wednesday against Santos, the Brazilian club, that starred Pele. The Santos backs were not ball winners but interceptors who stole the ball and then, with the craft of inside-forwards, put it where they wanted. Nish was the Brazilian type. He was flawless on the ball and a thoroughbred mover who could play either left- or right-back; we played him on the left, yet I often wondered if he might not have been even better on the other flank.

I'm a racing man and I've fallen into the habit of classifying footballers like horses – some are selling-platers and a rare few are classic hopes. Nish was a classic, although some critics regarded him as a luxury. Brian and I believed he was the sort of luxury every successful team can afford, because he provided extra possession at the back and initiated brainier build-ups. We didn't worry about the dangers of those build-ups breaking down; that didn't happen often.

David Nish (and I know he won't be offended) wouldn't get into our list of the 100 best tacklers, but I know who would top it. Henry Newton was one of those quiet, inoffensive types with a pitiless streak; he is probably the strongest tackler I've seen and certainly the best that Brian and I have managed. Henry joined us by a roundabout route from Forest

– he had to spend two years at Everton. We had been too successful with our signings from Nottingham, and Forest's new chairman Tony Wood, now an Arsenal director, seemed anxious to block deals between us.

Our approach to Forest for Newton in October 1970 was so obstructed that we were unable to agree a fee. Years later, Henry told us that he was taken to meet an Everton delegation after receiving this threat in Nottingham: 'If you don't sign for them, some nasty things might come out. For instance, that you've been tapped by Clough and Taylor.' Henry ought to have challenged his accusers, he ought to have shown anger and demanded to see their evidence; instead, never being the type to cause a scene, he signed without protest.

The Newton veto was a minor irritation compared to the furore over our attempt to sign Ian Storey-Moore. In my opinion, Forest cheated us out of his signature and their actions soured relationships between the clubs for years. Storey-Moore was a versatile England forward who could slot into attacks at left, right or centre. He was fast and could finish. Forest were going nowhere at the time; they needed some money and unloading Ian, who was twenty-eight, seemed the way to raise £200,000. Manchester United made an offer. We matched it and Matt Gillies, Forest's manager, phoned us to say, 'Now it's up to the player.' We were talking terms with him within forty minutes of that call.

United's manager Frank O'Farrell believed that Storey-Moore was a certainty for Old Trafford, but we can be very persuasive and Ian signed for us. He signed not once, but seven times. He trusted us so completely that he signed all the documents blank, leaving Derby County to fill in the terms. He had been won over by the sheer common sense of Brian's message: 'At twenty-eight, which is more important – going to United and beginning a rebuilding or completing a Derby team that can win the League Championship this season?'

The sports pages next morning announced, 'Derby snatch Moore', but O'Farrell refused to accept defeat and found eager allies in Forest's committee room. A deal that had seemed copper-bottomed began springing leaks; some influential people in football, not just those in Nottingham, appeared to be ranged against us. Forest dug up a technical objection, claiming, 'The transfer is incomplete because the forms have not been signed by our club secretary, Ken Smales.' What a piddling complaint! A club secretary's signature on a transfer form was only a rubber stamp and we had signed dozens of players without bothering about secretaries.

Brian sent the league a four-page telegram protesting against Forest's action; meanwhile, we tried to bluff it out by inviting Ian Storey-Moore to the Baseball Ground on Saturday afternoon. We paraded him round the pitch as Derby's latest signing; technically he wasn't, nor did he ever become our player. The signature of Ken Smales was withheld from the transfer forms, allowing O'Farrell to re-negotiate. So Ian Storey-Moore signed for Manchester United, but, without him, we still won the championship in 1971–72. He must have felt sick about missing that!

The league fined Derby £5,000 for 'a breach of transfer regulations' in parading Ian Storey-Moore as our player when his registration was still held by Forest. More seriously, a joint FA and league commission found Derby County guilty in April 1970 of 'gross negligence in the administration' and imposed the heaviest penalties in the history of English football at the time. The club were fined £10,000 and banned for a year from taking their place in the Fairs Cup (the forerunner of the UEFA Cup) and from arranging friendlies against foreign teams.

The chief plank in the case against Derby was a payment of £2,000 to Dave Mackay Ltd for programme articles; it meant only £20 per article but the league had warned against entering into the arrangement. Derby was also found guilty of failing to lodge the contracts of three players with the league and, against the rules, of varying the contracted payments to players during the season.

Now, I cannot pretend innocence on the list of eight charges, but Brian and I felt that the book had been thrown at us. Every technicality was dug up; for instance, that lodging allowances had been paid to our apprentice professionals instead of directly to their landladies. We believed the severity of the punishment reflected our unpopularity with the authorities and Brian, when addressing a lunch of the Sports Writers' Association, was frank about his strained relationship with league secretary Alan Hardaker, saying, 'Trouble has blown up because I've been so open in my criticism of him. It seems you cannot say that he has too much power.'

1970 was not a good year for my health, either. In fact, I'd suffered a heart attack without knowing it – I thought it was indigestion. I was taken ill on our coach ride from a Paddington hotel to Arsenal at the end of October 1970. I felt so awful that I lay down on the treatment table, saying to Brian, 'I'd give anything to stay here.' Instead, I dragged myself to the dug-out for the match and then engaged in travelling arrangements that could have killed me. The team, with me in charge, were off to Majorca next day on a winter break, so I returned to Derby, went home to pack, then travelled by road to Luton Airport and flew at three in the morning.

Somehow I survived and suffered no more pain until the night before a home match against Wolves two months later. I phoned Brian at half past seven in the morning, waking him to say, 'You won't see me today. I've not slept a wink, I feel like death and I think I've got cancer.'

He said, 'Be at the ground in an hour.'

'It's no good,' I said, 'I've had it.'

He repeated, 'I want you here not later than nine.'

Such is the force of Brian's personality that I dragged myself there, unaware how busily he had pulled strings in the meantime. The X-ray department of the nearest hospital had agreed to open for me on what was supposed to be their weekend off, a doctor had been persuaded to come in and check the plates and a specialist in the town had granted an immediate appointment. I knew before we reached the specialist's consulting rooms that cancer was not my trouble; the X-rays had cleared me and, besides, he was known throughout Derby as a heart man.

'You've had an attack, probably about eight weeks ago,' he said. I told him about my day in London and he said, 'That fits. Now drive home very slowly and stay there.'

I tried to explain, 'It's Saturday morning. Brian Clough is waiting outside and we have a match against Wolves.'

'Mr Taylor,' he said, 'you have no match, nor will you have for several weeks. It's important that you rest completely.'

So I stayed home, reading *Raceform* and watching TV, where every weekend seemed to produce outbursts from Brian. His practice at public speaking, his knack of being able to talk for an hour without notes and his fearlessness had combined to make him a TV natural, but I began to feel he was abusing the platform while, at the same time, the programme bosses were exploiting him. It seemed he was being urged into ever-greater controversies; it was inevitable that Brian and the unvarnished truth would create enemies in high places, and, as events earlier in the year had indicated, we had enough of those already.

Many of them must have been eager to believe that a terrible blunder had been made in paying a record fee for Todd. Certainly our results through March, Colin's first full month with us, supported that view because we picked up only one point and lost to Leeds, Liverpool, Newcastle and Forest. So we finished a moderate ninth in that 1970–71 season, which is best remembered for Arsenal's league and FA Cup double. Who could have guessed then that we would supplant them as champions a year later?

CHAPTER 8

THE WIDENING RIFT

Brian was in the Scilly Isles when we won the championship; I was in Majorca. And the police were on the prowl! Football buzzed with rumours of an attempt to fix a match that would have cost us that 1971–72 league title. It was a re-arranged game: Wolves *v.* Leeds United, who had won the FA Cup only two days earlier. Leeds needed only a draw to clinch the rare league and cup double. Liverpool, the other championship challengers, needed a win that same night at Arsenal. Our fixtures had been completed a week earlier and we topped the table but the bookies didn't believe we would stay there, offering 5–1 against us for the title.

It was logical to regard us as out of the running because Arsenal, beaten in the final by Leeds, would probably be in the dumps and no test for Liverpool, while Leeds, as Wembley victors, ought to be stoked up for the double. Logic, once again, was stood on its head. Liverpool could only draw and Leeds lost 2–1, but Wolverhampton CID still investigated allegations of bribes being offered to some of the Wolves players.

Bill McGarry, manager of Wolves and one of the straightest men in football, warned his team that the whispers made it particularly important to give their best, as they did. A team talk isn't needed when a manager is able to say in the dressing room, 'If you lose tonight, the supporters will believe that you're bent.' John Gow, the Swansea referee who handled the match, says, 'Anyone who suggests that the Wolves were bribed doesn't know what they're talking about. It was one of my hardest games for years. There was so much at stake, a lot of tension and no way that Wolves would concede defeat.'

Yet Leeds were denied a first-half penalty that would probably have presented them with the title. Mr Gow says, 'A handling offence was recorded in the assessor's report. It happened on my blind side and there was a loud appeal. I looked to my linesman but he didn't signal anything, so we carried on. No one contacted me before the match with advice on how to run the game, and that suggestion is rubbish. I'd no idea that an investigation would be held and the police have never been in touch with me.'

The detectives found no evidence to support the allegations and the inquiry was dropped. Derby, meanwhile, was

launched on the biggest party since VE Day. Fans presented us with a cake iced as a replica of the Baseball Ground,
complete with floodlight pylons. We were feted at dinners
and receptions; at one of these functions, Brian paid me a
particularly warm tribute: 'Peter's the man who gets me up at
six to go after players; who puts ideas into practice while I'm
still thinking of them; who tells the team what great players
they are after I've given them a rocket, and who smokes all
my cigarettes.'

Even as the corks popped, we sensed that our honeymoon
with Derby County might be ending, although neither of us
foresaw the public meetings, the writs and threatened strike
by the players over our tumultuous departure some sixteen
months hence. Our relationship with the directors had broken
down by then. It started to sour even while we were winning
the league. Little things started the trouble; for instance, a
remark to me about a £14,000 signing.

He was Roger Davies, a centre-forward from Worcester
City in the Southern League. I watched him three times and
offered £6,000, but Worcester's board was dominated by two
brothers, who were builders and shrewd businessmen. They
pushed up the price to £14,000 in September 1971. Arsenal,
Coventry City and Portsmouth were in the hunt but seemed
to want Davies on trial when, to our way of thinking, success
in transfers comes from decisions backed with instant cash.

To quote Brian on himself, 'Decisiveness is my greatest quality; I've taken more decisions in five years than some managers take in their careers.'

I watched Davies for the third time, then phoned Brian from a call box near the Worcester ground, 'It's definitely yes.' He drove over and the deal was set up that Saturday night, but the pleasure from this little scoop was marred by Sam Longson. We were back at Derby with the ink barely dry on the transfer forms when the chairman carped to me, 'I hope you're right; £14,000 is a lot for a non-league player.' I told him, 'Go to hell,' and I walked out of the ground. A professional ought not to be needled by criticism from an amateur, but I allowed the timing of Sam's remark and the sarcasm of his tone to get under my skin.

My strength lay in assessing players, and Longson had attacked my judgement. I resented that after spending three weeks in weighing up Davies. Every transfer is fraught with risks, but we had never put a foot wrong in the market and we had enough in the bank to cover the £14,000 fee a dozen times over. The team were riding high, so I didn't think that anyone had the right to question me. Brian said later, 'You shouldn't let the chairman upset you,' and I knew he was right. I'm aware, too, that I can make mistakes just like anyone else in the transfer market and mistakes are more likely to occur if doubts are cast by the very people who ought to be backing you. So I flared up at Sam, instead of explaining calmly that Davies represented potential. He was only twenty-one, a six-footer and a striker (they are always scarce), so it was unimportant that we had been compelled to double our offer. Indeed, Derby sold Davies some four years later for nearly £200,000.

While I was boiling about Sam Longson and directors generally, I remembered how the Derby board quibbled over the £110,000 fee for Terry Hennessey when they should have asked only, 'What's the best way to raise the money?' It's an old story in football. A manager reduces the overdraft, improves playing standards and brightens the club's prospects – and then the directors, who had been hiding while he did the hard work, start sticking an oar in and deluding themselves that they can run the club without a professional in full control.

Brian lashed this attitude in a speech to the shareholders when he said, 'The threat to me comes from the faceless, nameless men with long knives who operate behind closed doors.'

Although it was October 1973 before we quit, we would have gone earlier if the board had ever dared to interfere with our handling of the team. We weren't frightened of resigning; we knew that we were in demand and would not be out of work for long. We weren't the most popular pair inside our own profession, because we were both opinionated and successful, and that's an annoying combination; but the dislike from other managers hardly mattered when weighed against the admiration of chairmen like Derrick Robins of Coventry City.

Robins was the Concrete King, a self-made millionaire and a football progressive. Coventry City, under his leadership and the managership of Jimmy Hill, climbed from the Fourth Division to the First – and, except for a short-lived appearance in the 1970 European Fairs Cup, have plodded around in mid-table since 1967. Yet, as I knew from nine years at Highfield Road, the continued presence of Coventry in the First Division was a feat because the city lacked a united feeling for football. It was populated largely by migrant car workers and we were often outshouted by opposition fans on our own ground.

Two serious approaches from Robins proved to us that we had something special to offer. If only he had been more patient, we might have joined Coventry City when he was seeking a successor to manager Noel Cantwell in March 1971. He pressed us for a decision and laid down a deadline; we asked him to extend it because Derby were running for the title. He refused, so that was that.

We never discouraged offers; it was good for our standing and self-confidence to be in demand, and some of the approaches were highly interesting. For instance, I remember the consortium of north-east businessmen who planned to install Brian and myself at Roker Park in December 1969, but the scheme failed because the Sunderland board refused to make way for them. Personally, I was disappointed when nothing came of negotiations in April 1970 with Clifford Coombs, the chairman of Birmingham City. He was a gentleman and I fancied working for him.

Uniquely in football management, the Foreign Secretary himself acted as our adviser about an enormous overseas offer. The job was running the Greek national team and would have paid nearly £20,000 each for three years, plus signing-on fees of around £10,000 each, and mostly tax-free. This was in March 1970, when Greece was in the grip of a military government known as 'the Colonels'. They were pro-British and recruited several league managers and coaches to run club sides in Athens and Thessaloniki. Their official representative came to the Baseball Ground with nine air tickets, saying, 'Come over with your families for a few days. See for yourselves, then make a decision.'

The Foreign Secretary was George Brown, now Lord George Brown. He was the MP for Belper, a Derbyshire constituency, and a first-name friend to us. George, accompanied always by his detective, was a regular Derby spectator and, being Labour, got on better with us than with the directors.

It's no secret that he enjoys a drink and we are always pleased to have a few glasses with him after matches. That's how we could cut through the red tape and bypass official channels when we needed to. We met in a quiet room at the Mackworth Hotel in Derby and talked for two hours. We explained that, as it meant taking our families, we needed guidance on the political situation in Greece and I think Brian had reservations about how long a hard-line regime would tolerate his outspoken nature.

George Brown contacted the British Ambassador in Athens on our behalf and the gist of the advice was, 'Be careful.' The Foreign Secretary didn't tell us not to go, but he pointed out the risk of another upset in Greece because the colonels were less secure than we imagined. Events proved him right within a couple of years but, at the time, I wanted to see for myself. Indeed, Lilian and I had packed our bags and were ready to leave for the airport when Brian decided, 'It's all off; I'm not meddling with dynamite.' The negotiations had dragged on for six weeks. A day after the final breakdown we received a cable from George Gedes, the president of the Greek FA, saying, 'We request you to consider that our proposal was never made,' but that was just face-saving. The deal was called off at our end, not at theirs.

The thought of new employers constantly round the corner kept up our spirits as the split widened between ourselves and the Derby board during the 1972–73 season. It began, as in the remark about Roger Davies, over a triviality. I can trace the origin of the great Derby bust-up directly to a boardroom objection about Brian's wish to take his wife and children on a pre-season tour of Holland and West Germany in August 1972. He knew my feeling that families and football tours don't mix, but they had travelled with us before and no one had minded. This time, though, contrary opinions were voiced rather bluntly by the directors and Brian took offence. He refused to go on the tour. That was how the rift started.

I don't know who said what in the board meeting, but I cannot avoid linking the opposition to Brian with the arrival of a director called Jack Kirkland. It's said that you should speak no ill of the dead, but I cannot bring myself to write anything kind about Mr Kirkland. I met him first at Doncaster races, disliked him immediately and forever thought of him as 'the big noise from Belper', where he had made a pile in plant-hire. He wanted to dictate and dominate, although he had not been in big football for five minutes. He was full of catchphrases. 'If you can't stand the heat, then get out of the kitchen' was a favourite; so was 'Fat people are lazy people', which, being on the heavy side myself, I found tactless.

But the gulf between us was really over his commitment to a dream of turning the Baseball Ground into a sports complex, and I knew that could be done only at the expense of the team. He snapped at me once, 'One more big signing, and that's your lot.' I tried to tell him, 'The influx of players into a club must never stop,' but it was like talking to a wall.

Groups of men rarely remain united for long; differences are inevitable and football boards are especially prone to form factions. Nor is it always sweetness and harmony between managerial partners. I've had some serious rows with Brian. The first was early in 1971 after discovering that I was not receiving anything like my fair share of the cake. Sam Longson had slipped Brian a £5,000 rise without offering me a penny.

I tackled Longson, saying, 'It's absolutely criminal.' He answered, 'Where did you get your information?' and that made me even angrier. Instead of asking questions, the pair of them should have been apologising; Longson for paying the money on the sly and Brian for accepting it and leaving me in the dark for eighteen months. That row cleared the air and we've not had a disagreement since over salaries, but we've clashed on other matters; most spectacularly, I'm ashamed to say, in front of the players before a European Cup semi-final in April 1973.

We occupied a quiet hotel in the hills outside Turin while the main party – the directors, the press and prominent supporters – stayed in the city where Stuart Webb, the club secretary, had arranged a dinner for the journalists, with Brian as chief speaker. I was due to attend but not to speak because, in those days, I was nervous about facing reporters or cameras and microphones. I've overcome my fears now to a certain extent but can never be as fluent or as natural as Brian. He's a master of communication; I'm not. So I was annoyed on coming downstairs, dressed to leave for the restaurant, to find Brian in his tracksuit and still playing in a card school that had started after lunch. He dismissed me over his shoulder, 'You go, Peter. On your own.'

I exploded, I lost my head. I called him a swine, I called him every imaginable name. Then I stormed up the stairs and went to bed. Next morning, having calmed down, I realised that we were both in the wrong – Brian for not being ready and, as I saw it, throwing me to the lions; myself for committing the worse offence of causing a vocal riot in the presence of players on the eve of a big match.

Turin was a bad city for me. The following afternoon I was arrested at the stadium after a row with two Germans. They were Gerhard Schulenberg, who was refereeing the first leg of our semi-final against Juventus, and Helmut Haller, who played for West Germany against England in the 1966 World Cup final and was now a sub for the Italian champions.

John Charles had travelled with us from Derby as the club's adviser. He was the giant Welshman who played half a dozen seasons as centre-forward for Juventus and is still revered throughout the province of Piedmont. Big John popped into our dressing room about half an hour before the kick-off to warn us, 'Haller's in with the ref again. That's twice I've seen him.'

No one connected with the competing clubs should enter a referee's room and John was right to tell us; indeed, since that day, we have always stationed someone to watch the referee's door in European matches. However, there was nothing we could do then except nurture our suspicions, which were further aroused at half-time when Haller walked off with the referee, instead of with his teammates. I hurried after them, trying to overhear and saying, 'I speak German, gentlemen. Do you mind if I listen?' Haller answered by jabbing me in the ribs with his elbow and, as I gasped for air, barked something that brought a squad of heavies into action.

They shoved me against a wall and kept me there. I didn't know who they were, except that some were uniformed, and possibly club stewards, and others looked like plain-clothes police. I didn't know what was going on; my only thought was, 'Let me get into that refs room because I've rumbled them.' John Charles towered up, first calling to me, 'Don't let them take your passport,' and then, through his impressive presence and immense prestige, calming the Juventus minders in fluent Italian. They released me, but not until the teams were filing out for the second half.

I know there is not a shred of evidence that Haller and

Schulenberg were engaged in anything improper or talking on any other basis than that of fellow countrymen glad to meet in a strange land. But, in the circumstances, their association was unwise and bound to cause adverse comment, particularly so when harsh bookings in the second half ruled out Roy McFarland and Archie Gemmill from the return leg. We drew the second leg 0–0 at Derby and ran into more trouble when Roger Davies was sent off, so the tie was lost 3–1 on aggregate.

The trouble in Turin continued after the match when Brian – insisting on a translation by the novelist and *Sunday Times* columnist Brian Glanville, who speaks perfect Italian – ordered away the local journalists from our dressing room with the words, 'I will not speak to cheating bastards.'

Italian clubs can blame only themselves for the widespread distrust of their relationships with referees; they are sometimes excessively generous to match officials and, in 1978, a Scottish referee and his linesmen were suspended for accepting a bonanza of shoes, shirts, ties, tracksuits, anoraks, waistcoats and scarves from AC Milan. UEFA, which fined Milan £8,000 for taking the three Scots on a shopping spree, stated, 'Bribery is not intended; it is simply that Southern European clubs are naturally hospitable.' Northern clubs don't view it so complacently; they fear that referees may be influenced by Latin generosity and I believe the only solution would be to ban any pre-match contact between the match officials and the clubs.

It was little consolation that Juventus failed in the final, losing 1–0 in Belgrade to Ajax Amsterdam, who thus completed a hat-trick of European Cup victories. I don't know if Derby County might have fared better against Ajax striker Johan Cruyff and his brilliant team, but at least an appearance in the final would have banished the gloom from a season dogged with disappointment from winning only one of our first six league matches.

CHAPTER 9

RESIGNATION AND ITS AFTERMATH

Sometimes I wish that 1973 had been wiped off the calendar. It was a year of troubles for us and the shemozzles in Turin were far from the worst of them. The climax, of course, came in the autumn with uproar over our resignations from Derby County.

Brian had kicked off the New Year controversially with his speech at a dinner honouring Peter Lorimer, the Leeds United and Scotland forward. I did not attend because I had cut down on functions since my heart attack two years ago. Five hundred guests, including Labour's leader Harold Wilson, were kept waiting while Brian disappeared to the lavatory. Then he began with these words: 'Despite the fact that Peter Lorimer falls when he has not been kicked and protests when he has nothing to protest about...' The rest of his address was interrupted by jeers and the scrape of chairs as angry Leeds fans walked out. Brian, of course, was unrepentant and countered accusations of rudeness by suggesting, 'Next time they should invite Basil Brush.'

Nor was Brian popular at the league headquarters at Lytham St Annes. And a poll of the ninety-two boardrooms would have shown equally little support for him there too. Football directors are mainly Conservatives, so they probably disapproved of him when he later gave match tickets to striking miners and offered to join the pickets in the coal dispute of February 1972.

The fuse was finally lit through Brian's dislike of Don Revie, the consistently successful manager of Leeds United. The deep-rooted cynicism of Revie's character and tactics is now nationally known and has been commented upon in the High Court, but Brian was first and foremost of Don's critics and made him the butt of such outrageous comments as, 'You have to listen carefully to what Don says, and think about it. Then either swallow it, or bring it up.'

Yet that was almost a mild observation compared with Brian's eruption after a meeting by the FA's disciplinary committee in the summer of 1973. They considered the record of Leeds United during the previous season and found them guilty of 'persistent misconduct on the field'. They fined Leeds £3,000 but then suspended the fine for a year, while imposing a censure.

Remembering our treatment in 1970, Brian thundered against 'the FA's befuddled minds', saying:

> Leeds should have been instantly relegated after being branded as one of the dirtiest clubs in Britain.
>
> I feel strongly that the tuppence-ha'penny suspended fine is the most misguided piece of woolly thinking ever perpetrated by the FA, a body hardly noted for its common sense. It's like breathalysing a drunken driver, getting a positive reading, giving him his keys back and telling him to watch it on the way home.

Those strong quotes appeared in the *Sunday Express* of August 1973 and the balloon went up when the eyes of officialdom reached the paragraph that said, 'The whole trouble with soccer's disciplinary system is that some of those who sit in judgement, being officials of other clubs, might well have a vested interest.'

That did it! The FA announced an investigation and let it be understood that Brian could hardly escape a charge of bringing the game into disrepute. Chairman Sam Longson began to fear that Derby County might be expelled from the league; he had listened for more than a year to other chairmen, FA councillors and members of the league management committee urging him to curb Clough.

Brian, though, was more outspoken than ever and a magnet for the cameras. He turned down £18,000 a year to succeed Jimmy Hill as ITV's soccer analyst but kept a regular Saturday platform with London Weekend's programme *On the Ball*.

Derby's board tried to gag Brian. He refused to be restrained, so the directors delivered an ultimatum to 'stop engaging in literary work by writing articles in the press and stop entering into commitments with radio and television'. The letter was signed by Sam Longson. We read it together and immediately resigned together. I saw our position as the outcome of Brian's false relationship with the chairman, something I had warned Brian about for years.

Sam Longson liked to pose as a homespun, small-town businessman, when he was really a haulage millionaire and a tough character who knew how to be devious when necessary – but, outside his own parish, he was a nobody until Brian and I joined Derby County. Sam was smart enough to concede this himself, by saying after the parting of our ways, 'I've got to be very fair and say that Brian Clough helped to make me. Who'd have heard of Sam Longson all over the country but for what Clough achieved?'

In my opinion, Longson used Brian to make himself a somebody and then turned on him. I watched how he cultivated Brian in the early days, saying, 'Can I go with you to

Arsenal?' or 'Will you introduce me to Sir Matt Busby?' – that sort of thing. I remember how Sam drove Brian to the television studios in Birmingham because he realised that every shot of Brian's face advertised Derby County. Sam lapped up the publicity and the exposure; for years he was part and parcel of the activities that he now wanted to stop. In my view, he was out of order.

I say that, because the club was not suffering from Brian's TV and newspaper crusades; on the contrary, the team opened that 1973–74 season with their best start in our six years at Derby. Longson, though, was blind to the table. He couldn't see the indisputable evidence of 'played seven, won four, drawn two, lost one', because he had switched allegiances. He had turned from Brian to the hierarchy of football; he had aligned himself with fellow chairmen, with people nearer his own age of seventy-two.

A switch like that was always possible and many times I warned Brian, 'Never get involved with a director socially; just keep it as a working relationship.' He didn't listen to me. He was too often at Sam's house with his children, allowing the chairman to buy them presents and not shrivelling with embarrassment when Longson kept referring to him publicly as 'my adopted son'.

I believe the objections to Brian's TV appearances were a red herring, camouflaging the intention of Longson and

Jack Kirkland to limit him. They were envious that he loomed larger than the board. Derby County was our club, not theirs. It was ours because we did the work. The directors did nothing except guarantee debts in the unlikely event of liquidation.

Yet we tried to reach a compromise by sending this letter to each director a month before our resignation:

> Due to the complete breakdown of communication, common sense and the ability to have a reasonable discussion with the chairman, we find it impossible to work with him for the good of Derby County any more. Would you please advise of the best way to resolve this urgent problem?

The only reply was a series of pin pricks. Our drinks cupboard was emptied one night and never restocked. I was refused permission to write for the *Derby Evening Telegraph*; our wives were denied their usual tickets to a match at Old Trafford; the club refused to cover our expenses for attending an international, Holland *v.* Poland, in Rotterdam; and, at the final showdown, we entered the boardroom to the graceless summons, 'Right, you two. Let's have you in.'

Some of the directors talked to us about an amicable financial settlement while, simultaneously, other directors and a lawyer were poring through our contracts to see if we had breached them. Longson, typically, rebuffed suggestions of a settlement. 'You're getting nowt,' he said, and I believed him. I knew the man and wasn't going to engage in a losing battle because the chairman's position was invulnerable. 'See out the contract and do as I say, or resign without compensation.' Anyone else might have paid us off, but not Sam Longson. Feelings had turned too bitter.

We had trebled Derby County's average attendances. We left them in third place in the First Division with £250,000 in the bank and a championship squad of players. We had steered them to the league title and into Europe, yet all Sam Longson could say as farewell was, 'Hand in your club-car keys on the way out.'

The board, as I saw it, double-dealt to the end, accepting Brian's resignation and then offering his job to me. They insulted me with their hope that I would rat on him.

Mike Keeling, the club's youngest director, resigned in sympathy with us and so did Brian's personal assistant, Cliff Notley. The townspeople rallied to our support and so did the players. The fury of their protests rocked the board.

I think many people were won over to our side by the revelations about the pettiness of the directors. Gerald Mortimer, chief sports writer of the *Derby Evening Telegraph*, told us, 'That trick of secretly emptying and locking your drinks cupboard was pulled on Harry Storer here when the board wanted to force him out.'

Our resignation notices were typed by Gerald as a favour, because we didn't want to embarrass the girl who did the club's typing, but he told us straight, 'I'm doing it although I don't agree with it. I believe you should stay and fight.' He voiced the majority view; everyone, except the board, wanted us to stay and a 'Bring Back Clough' movement was formed and coordinated by Don Shaw, a playwright, and Bill Holmes, an industrial manager. They booked halls throughout Derbyshire for protest meetings.

The first home match, five days after our resignations, demonstrated the enormous support for us. The players, who had talked of striking, decided to play first and protest afterwards. The fixture, nominally Derby County *v.* Leicester City, was really Sam Longson *v.* Brian Clough. Extra police were on duty and plain-clothes men guarded the board, although the only violence was the tossing of two paper cups into the directors' box.

Banners proclaimed, 'Clough is King' and 'Longson out, Clough in', and the terraces thundered approval when Brian appeared. He had borrowed a season ticket for a seat only a few yards from Longson, who tried to upstage him by standing in the directors' box and repeatedly thrusting his arms aloft as though the applause for Brian had been meant for the board. He fooled no one, possibly not even himself.

Brian watched only the opening few minutes and

then slipped away to where I was waiting in a chauffeur-driven Rolls. Parking restrictions and streets lined with empty double-decker buses had forced us to stop some distance from the ground, so Brian had to run from a pursuing pack of photographers. But, being fit and still only in his thirties, he outsped them easily. Our limousine then whisked us to London for an appearance on the *Michael Parkinson Show* that kept the pot boiling.

The King's Hall, the biggest indoor venue in Derby, was packed with some 700 protesters when Brian returned. They gave him a standing ovation and he broke down.

The players asked to meet us in a pub; instead, we took them, their wives and children as our guests to a country hotel near my house. We bought them thirty bottles of champagne and talked over old times. The party was meant as a farewell but the players didn't want to say goodbye; skipper Roy McFarland handed this letter to Sam Longson the following morning:

> During the events of last week we, the undersigned players, have kept our feelings within the dressing room. However, at this time, we are unanimous in our support and respect for Mr. Clough and Mr. Taylor and ask that they be re-instated as manager and assistant manager of the club.
>
> It was absolutely vital that we won against Leicester on

Saturday for ourselves, as well as for the club and fans. Now that match is out of the way, nobody can say that we have acted on the spur of the moment and are just being emotional.

We called the meeting of first-teamers and it was emphasised that nobody was under obligation to attend. But everybody was there. We then decided to write this letter and again nobody was under pressure to sign. But again, everybody did.

The signatories were Colin Boulton, Ron Webster, David Nish, John O'Hare, Roy McFarland, Colin Todd, John McGovern, Archie Gemmill, Roger Davies, Kevin Hector, Alan Hinton and Steve Powell. Only the name of Henry Newton was missing, but he had been away in Lancashire on business. Henry was back, though, the following afternoon when the first-team squad invaded the club offices and besieged the boardroom in an uprising unparalleled in English football.

The players were furious about what they regarded as a brush-off from the board. There had been no answer to their letter so they rampaged through the Baseball Ground for three hours in search of one. Fists hammered on the boardroom door because they believed that all the directors were locked inside. In fact, only two men were hiding from the team's fury – director Jack Kirkland and the club secretary Stuart Webb, who confided afterwards that, through being unable to reach the toilet in the corridor, they pressed into service the board's champagne bucket.

Chairman Longson was safely away from the siege. He was in Nottingham signing a manager to right the capsizing ship, a man whose name commanded respect both in the dressing room and in the streets of Derby. He was Forest's boss, our old star Dave Mackay.

I welcomed Mackay's appointment; I wanted the hysteria to die down – but that was a forlorn hope. The uproar had thrown the team out of its stride; we were into the New Year before they again played to their true ability.

Bad results fuelled the protest movement and the club's annual meeting, in December 1973, wasn't far short of a riot. Pickets chanted abuse at chief shareholder Jack Kirkland and, inside the meeting, Sam Longson became so agitated under hostile questioning that he confused the microphone with a hearing aid and held it to his ear. Probably nothing illustrates the bitterness of feeling more than Longson's threat at this meeting to Mike Keeling, ex-director and leader of the protest movement: 'I have four men here who'll pick you up, throw you down the stairs and kick you into the street!'

I didn't share Brian's warm feelings towards the protesters. It was pleasing to be the object of such loyalty and yet I felt the movement was misdirected and a losing cause. I said to

Brian, 'We've resigned and that's it. We're never going back, so we shouldn't mislead people.'

But the protesters organised themselves so effectively that Mackay was complaining a full year later, 'Between 2,000 and 3,000 people are still staying away from every home match because of the Clough affair.' And there are quite a few fans in Derby who swear that Dave, even though winning the League Championship in 1974–75 with what was virtually our team, was never fully accepted as manager by the terraces.

CHAPTER 10

HOLLOW VICTORY

After such an uproar, who could have imagined the dawning of a day when Derby County's directors would beg us to return?

They ought to have been sick of the names Clough and Taylor. We had lambasted them in the media. We had roused the town against them and cost the club a fortune in lost receipts. We had set up shop together, eventually, only sixteen miles away at Nottingham Forest and stolen Derby County's headlines. And, in addition, Brian had forced the board to pay £24,000 as an out-of-court settlement of a libel action.

Football is such a desperate business, though, that face-saving always runs a bad second to the hunger for success. So the Derby board swallowed this series of humiliations and, in February 1977, surrendered almost unconditionally by inviting us back to the Baseball Ground in our old jobs.

We discussed the offer with them and then, largely because of Brian's personal loyalty to the Forest vice-chairman Stuart Dryden, turned it down. 'I'm not a penny better off as a result of this decision,' Brian told the world afterwards, which was true.

Derby came for us because they feared relegation to the Second Division. Dave Mackay had won the 1974–75 League Championship with a team formed mostly of players inherited from us. Then decline set in and people around the club began to feel that Mackay, such a battler on the pitch, wasn't energetic enough in his measures to arrest it. He and assistant manager Des Anderson were sacked and the team drifted for two months under the reserve team trainer Colin Murphy, an FA coach with no playing experience in big-time football.

A new power had risen in the Derby boardroom – 48-year-old George Hardy, who had become acting chairman after only two years as a director. Hardy was a former car salesman who had prospered in scrap metal and in building. He drove a Ferrari and a Rolls-Royce. He had the bright idea of approaching former Liverpool manager Bill Shankly to become consultant manager of Derby. And he admired us.

Hardy had backed a £330,000 gamble (a record fee at the time) on the Charlton Athletic striker Derek Hales, who was bearded, burly and brave – but, as Brian and I could have warned Derby, without the technique to pierce First Division

defences. He scored in only one of his first ten league matches and the club's position became serious. That's why the
directors abased themselves – which I don't think is too
strong a word – in asking Forest for permission to approach
us. Apparently the idea of a reconciliation had always been in
Hardy's mind; he hadn't been on the board at the time of our
resignation and regarded our going as a calamity.

I was interested in Derby's approach because the Baseball
Ground has always appealed to me. Nottingham is my birth-
place but I feel more at home in Derby, a real football town.
I am sure that, under the urgings of Mr Hardy, a majority of
directors were sincere in wanting us back, and yet I felt there
were some political angles to the offer. Our return would dis-
band the protest movement, still active after more than three
years. All the directors wanted the protesters pacified, and I
believe that a few of them may also have calculated that our
return would not merely curb the power of Sam Longson,
but oust him.

Longson's resignation from the board would have been our
first condition; we couldn't work with him, so he would have
to go. And he did lose the chairmanship when the directors
voted 5–1 to approach us. Sam, who once used to carry a picture of Brian in his wallet, left almost in tears. Whatever my
personal feelings about Sam Longson, I recognise that he
always had at heart what he regarded as the best interests of

Derby County. He opposed our return on the grounds that it was undignified, as he put it, to 'go cap-in-hand for Brian Clough. Football doesn't begin and end with that man.'

Sam didn't resign his directorship and he retained the figurehead title of club president. But, for practical purposes, his sway was over and his annoyance with the board was complete when, in the end, we decided to stay with Forest. He finally left the board in May 1980 as the team were relegated; he said his health was poor.

'They've given me the sack,' he complained. 'It leaves a stigma against my name, yet I've done nothing to deserve it. And they've made a public spectacle of the club.'

Brian and I went back to the Baseball Ground to break the news of our decision; as Brian said, 'We could have phoned, but we had to look Mr Hardy in the face when we told him.'

From a distance, the episode looked like a 'game, set and match' type of revenge – Derby coming begging for us; Longson, our arch opponent, quitting the chair; and the final snub of the rejected offer. We didn't plan it, though. The events just happened and I would never wish to harm Derby County because my happiest times were there. I am disgusted by their relegation at the end of the 1979–80 season and bitter towards the men who caused it. The Baseball Ground meant more than just a job to me; I look at their new stand and remember how I had a heart attack in building the team that paid for it; I think of the decrepit condition of the club when Brian and I arrived and I fear that those depths will be plumbed again. I don't blame the managers who followed us; I don't blame Dave Mackay, or Colin Murphy, or Tommy Docherty or Colin Addison. They were not responsible for the original, disastrous decision which forced our resignations.

If we had stayed, Derby County would have won the European Cup long before Nottingham Forest and would still be among the premier clubs of England. They are back in the Second Division today because a few interfering directors imagined they could run the show. All Derby's troubles stem from that.

I think back to my many sleepless nights before the resignation and to Lilian's relief when the break became final. My wife never questions my actions in football and my children kept their opinions to themselves, but my family couldn't hide their surprise that such a major breach between board and management could have occurred at a club lying second in the table.

Barbara Clough attended a protest meeting a month after Brian had found a new job at Brighton, yet I guess she must have been as relieved as Lilian about the resignations; perhaps more relieved because the last six months were hell at Derby and Brian was always in the firing line, which I wasn't.

I have to guess because, strange as it may seem to fans,

Brian and I never socialise together nor visit each other's homes, and our wives met only once during the Derby bust-up. It was at the farewell party for the players where the mood was all against swapping stories of our troubles. We weren't downhearted that day; rather, we had a wonderful time reminiscing about some magnificent years. Everyone in that room, including ourselves, had prospered at Derby and the management techniques forged there have stood Brian and myself in good stead ever since.

We talked that night about Dave Mackay and young Roy McFarland and Kevin Hector nicking the goals and how their blend of experience, quality and pace, allied to the drive of Willie Carlin, helped us to run away with the Second Division.

We remembered how, a year later, as the second highest scorers in the First Division, we qualified for the Watney Cup and won 4–1 in the final by walloping the famous Manchester United of Bobby Charlton, Denis Law and George Best. We recalled our nineteen goals in four rounds when winning the Texaco Cup and, best of all, how we won the League Championship.

*　　*　　*

We watched the champagne corks flying and thought how success in football rests on a simple principle: find talent, then handle it. And handling it often requires ruthlessness, as was shown by our sale of Willie Carlin. He had been a vital component in the promotion team, had played a full season for us in the First Division and was an ever-present force through the first two months of the following season. Imagine his shock when I kept him at the ground after he had played in a Saturday match against Chelsea and introduced 'Mr Frank O'Farrell of Leicester City who has made an offer for you. We're willing to let you go.'

Willie's heart was broken and I believe he still hasn't forgiven me for selling him so abruptly. There's no pleasure in parting with a player who has given good service but the decisions have to be made, however painful. I considered that Willie was over the top, I thought Leicester's offer was reasonable and, being realistic, money in the bank was more useful than a veteran midfield player in our reserves.

I had the same painful decision when selling Archie Gemmill from Forest to Birmingham City in 1979. I knew that replacing him would be a problem because players with Archie's drive and eagerness for battle are always scarce; yet he was also into his thirties and we had seen the best of him, so Birmingham's offer of £150,000 was too attractive to refuse.

We unloaded Dave Mackay in the same way; Swindon paid us £20,000 and he became their manager. It's as important in football as in the stock market to sell at the right time.

Brian and I are noted for our signings but it shouldn't be overlooked that we have picked up some handy fees through selling. It's an unpopular part of management, but it has to be done. A manager should always be looking for signs of disintegration in a winning side and then sell the players responsible before their deterioration is noticed by possible buyers. It's something we put to players when signing them. We don't beat about the bush; we have the patter off by heart. It goes like this: 'Son, the first time we can replace you with a better player, we'll do it without blinking an eyelid. That's what we're paid to do – to produce the best side and to win as many things as we can. If we see a better player than you but don't sign him, then we're frauds. But we're not frauds and so just remember that anyone who plays for us can be replaced overnight.'

I've noticed over the years how often Liverpool sell players as they near or pass their thirtieth birthday. Bob Paisley believes the average First Division footballer is beginning to burn out at thirty; I wouldn't disagree with him, especially if the player has served ten years in a running side like Liverpool. They last a little longer in teams with our style of putting a foot on the ball and then pushing it about.

However, sometimes we sign players who are over thirty – Stan Bowles, for instance. He's a gambler, too, but that didn't scare us; I'm one myself. When we have a gambler in the club I'll go with him to the races because I know that simply saying 'stop' won't cure him. Yet we say no to team gambling and banned a school last season where the limit was only £1. Three-card brag is outlawed on the team bus; indeed, I dislike any form of gambling on the way to matches. If football-ers must play cards, it's best they start a game of something brainier than brag.

As well as gamblers, we've signed drinkers and provided them with booze under our supervision. We've signed chain smokers, too. We have a stock transfer question, to which we usually know the answer: 'Let's hear your vice before you sign – is it women, booze, drugs or gambling?' Footballers without a failing are rare, in my experience, and they need fathering through their problems.

When I sat down with Stan Bowles in December 1979, there was no need to put our stock question because his weakness has been well publicised, but I gave him the usual warning, 'When I tell you everything you may not want to sign for us. We operate as dictators and nothing is going to change us. We don't allow players to keep secrets from us; we don't allow players to talk out of turn. Any problem in your private life must be brought to us; you may not like that but we'll prove to you that our way of management is good for all of us.'

We stress to all our players, 'Worry off the field shows itself on the field and damages our aim of a maximum performance on match days, so it's a crime against the team to retain a problem. You must come to us, you must put your cards on the table. We have to know everything.' It's done in the strictest confidence, of course. I can never reveal the names of footballers who have poured out their hearts to Brian and myself about sexual, domestic, gambling and, in one case, religious troubles. If we couldn't find an answer, we would turn to experts; we have sought advice for our players from clergymen, doctors and local councillors.

I remember a player whose form began fluctuating mysteriously, and I realised he had a problem but couldn't put my finger on it. He was the last man I would associate with gambling and yet, when he finally confided in us, that was the trouble. He owed £1,500 and was being pushed for payment. We cleared off the debt immediately.

Outstanding results come from team meetings where nothing is barred, and Brian is thinking of them when he often talks of 'driving players to the very limit of their endurance; I humiliate them'. A fellow who has shown cowardice in a match, or lied to us, or broken our code of decent behaviour, would rather be taken to task in the privacy of the office. It's a terrible shock to him when his offence is paraded before a group of clubmates, and he is always careful not to err again.

Derby was the testing ground for our unconventional ideas

on training. We don't send players slogging up sandhills; we think relaxation is important in maintaining fitness. I remember an afternoon in the promotion season when our only training was driving dodgems at Blackpool; the following day, and on *Match of the Day*, we beat Blackpool 3–2.

Even players accustomed to Brian's unpredictability were amazed, though, when he suddenly produced crates of beer on Forest's coach trip to Liverpool for the second leg of the European Cup in 1978. We had won the first leg 2–0 and yet – and it's the worst insult we've suffered – everyone was writing us off. A poll of First Division managers showed that only three out of the twenty-two believed that we could hold our lead and eliminate Liverpool, the cup holders. The three were John Neal at Middlesbrough, Alan Dicks at Bristol City and Ken Shellito at Chelsea. The players had read that; they were annoyed and perhaps worried in case such a majority of managers might be right. So there was a lot of tension and we tried to disperse it by playing this big game down; we didn't bother travelling until the day of the game and we stowed beer on the coach like a pub team's outing.

It's laughable in a way, yet also shrewd psychology. The gates of Anfield, where even the strongest visitors quail, had been locked on a full-house crowd of about 52,000 for an hour before the kick-off. And where were Forest? Rolling along the motorway with Brian's bottle-opener working overtime as he pressed drinks on the team… 'Go on, have a beer! All right, well, have another. It'll relax you.' It worked. We drew o–o in one of the most disciplined displays in our time with Forest, and went on to win the European Cup ourselves in Munich at the end of the season.

Our ideas on fitness horrify many coaches. Their attitude is typified by Sammy Chung, who was the manager of Wolves until they sacked him in 1978 after another bad start to a season. Sammy, in his days as a club coach, turned up in Majorca where we were on a club holiday with Derby County. I was sunning myself on the beach when he asked, 'Who is your fittest player?' I nodded along the sands towards Colin Todd.

'I suppose Toddy's not bad.'

Sammy licked his lips… 'I could make him sick in three minutes; I could give him a programme that would put him on his back.'

'I wouldn't let you near him. He's a footballer, not a racehorse.'

Sammy, a very likeable lad even though he is a fitness nut, then repeated his challenge to Brian, 'I can make your fittest player physically sick inside three minutes.' And Brian squashed him by saying, 'When the league start awarding two points for that, we'll give you a job.'

Sammy came off worst in another exchange with Brian

on the same Cala Mayor beach another year. We were lying around while Sam, then the coach at Wolves after moving from Ipswich, was explaining to a foreigner the difference in England between managers and coaches. He was having trouble making himself clear. What we call a manager is called a trainer by Continentals, and what they call a manager we would call a secretary. Brian, half-raising himself from the deckchair beside me, interrupted Sammy and called to the foreigner, 'I'll tell you the difference between managers and coaches. It's ten heart attacks a year.'

The strain on managers is a topic that's guaranteed to draw a hot reaction from Brian. I've sat in dug-outs with him while he has swept an arm in the direction of the terraces and said, 'Not one of them out there understands what it's like to be us in here, watching eleven blokes run for our jobs. Even the players don't understand; once they've taken their boots off today, they've finished – but that's when our worrying starts.' I'll never forget his retort to a suggestion that he join the football managers' pension scheme: 'And it pays out when you're sixty-five? They must be bloody joking.'

*   *   *

Brian was looking forward to an escape from the pressures after we resigned from Derby; he talked of taking six months off and travelling the world before looking for another club. I disagreed; I wanted another job immediately, and I got my way when an offer came out of the blue.

Barely a fortnight after leaving Derby, we were back in business. The club was Brighton and Hove Albion, sixth from bottom of the Third Division, with average gates of only 6,000. Brian studied their team and summed up the problem in a sentence: 'We'll have to get some players with coal on their faces.'

CHAPTER 11

GOING SOLO AT BRIGHTON

Only the man on the end of the phone attracted me to Brighton. He was Mike Bamber, a property developer and the club chairman. He was persuasive, progressive and brave enough to make his move while the charge of bringing football into disrepute hung over Brian.

The FA disciplinary commission were to hear the case in a fortnight. At best, a long suspension was forecast and one First Division manager assured the ITV producer Bob Gardam, 'Those two will never get another club.' Bob, a good friend, was upset but I said, 'We've done no wrong. So go back and tell the fellow we'll have his job if he's not careful.' I could understand directors being wary and I could understand some of the Derby board stirring things up, but I objected to fellow managers putting in the boot while we were out of work. A couple of years later, that manager was sacked himself. We shed no tears for him.

I have a lot of time for Mike Bamber. He had heard the rumours but believed me when I told him, 'We have done nothing to prevent us taking any job in football. The gossip is rubbish.' We met late on Saturday night at the Waldorf Hotel in London. Brian and I had been in the ITV studios watching Derby draw against West Ham, while Mr Bamber had been in Hereford seeing his team lose 4–0 and hearing more abuse from Brighton supporters. He arrived with the vice-chairman Harry Bloom; they meant business and we were impressed.

Brian, though, was set on a long break but I pushed him into accepting the offer. He agreed but his heart wasn't in it – as events were to show. Yet he summoned up the old bounce on our first day at Brighton's Goldstone Ground. This was Brian at his most quotable: 'It's tougher here than at Hartlepools where they didn't expect anything. Now we have a reputation, but there are no fairies at the bottom of Brighton pier. There are only sixteen professionals here. Only one goalkeeper, one trainer, one secretary, one groundsman; in fact, one of everything. That puts Peter and me in the majority, for they have two managers.'

The fans could also produce bright remarks and I heard them saying, 'Fetching Clough and Taylor to Brighton is like engaging McAlpines to decorate a roadside cafe.' I saw what they meant when I met the team at a hotel in Lewes. They were casual, almost amateurish, joking about their plight instead of being concerned. Brian thrust his chin at them, challenging, 'Go on, punch it! Show me you're capable of positive action.' I wanted to wade in, too, but decided that the best course was wholesale replacement.

Our outstanding result in November 1973 was at the disciplinary hearing. I attended with Brian and the commission cleared him. We were free to work and I've rarely worked harder. I was away scouting while Brian's hands were full trying to explain away some awful defeats. We lost 4–0 in an FA Cup replay to an amateur club, Walton and Hersham. We lost 8–2 at home in the league to Bristol Rovers. It wasn't our team, but that was no consolation. Brian tried to draw the blame on himself by saying, 'The players seem petrified of me. They put on a shirt, look at me and wonder if they're doing it right. It's got to change or we'll go down.'

Brian, although his heart and home remained in Derby, wanted to win for Brighton. He yearned for success, as he always does. There's a delightful story about that from John Vinicombe, who covers all Brighton matches for the *Evening Argus*. He inadvertently opened the dressing room door at Walsall after the first away victory under our management – and found Brian, on his knees, untying the players' boots.

Meanwhile, the cauldron still bubbled at Derby. The players signed another letter demanding our reinstatement, while threatening not to report for a match against Leeds United. I was too busy travelling to take much interest; one night I was standing in the crowd at Chester, the next night I was more than 200 miles away watching Norwich reserves. My job is: observation, decision, replacement. It wasn't difficult at Brighton to see who to replace.

My first signing was the veteran goalkeeper Peter Grummitt from Sheffield Wednesday for only £7,000. Next, John Bond of Norwich City agreed a package deal of £65,000 for three of his reserves: Andy Rollings, Ian Mellor and Steve Govier. Rollings was still in the side when Brighton won promotion to the First Division in 1979. He was a defender, as was Govier. I paid Luton Town £20,000 for Ken Goodeve, another defender. We got it right at the back, so we stayed up in 1973–74 – and I was glad, because I had fallen for Brighton. I loved the club, the people and the place, but Brian never took to the south coast. We weren't a unit at Brighton. His mind was elsewhere; he hankered after Derby for a long time. He had tasted championship football and couldn't adjust to the Third Division.

Brighton, still fighting relegation in the New Year, went off to Cambridge for a match, while Brian flew to New York for a fight between Muhammad Ali and Joe Frazier. He met

Ali who taunted, 'Hey, you a football player in England? You wouldn't last two minutes over here, you're too small' – which only goes to show that the champ had never heard of soccer. He thought the only kind of football was gridiron which, of course, is played by giants.

Brian returned from America only to start planning a cricket trip to the West Indies in February. Then he flew to Tehran in March to discuss an offer from the Shah of £20,000 a year tax-free for us as joint managers of the Iranian national team. He also left the team to canvass in the Midlands during the 1974 general election. And he never discouraged the offers that poured in: from Ajax Amsterdam, from Aston Villa, from Queens Park Rangers. I didn't want to work in Iran or Holland or anywhere except Brighton because Mike Bamber, realising the club's potential, was prepared to back his judgement with cash. He wanted the best, he was ready to pay, and he was determined to enforce his five-year contract with Brian – but I knew that a split was inevitable.

Brian's absences began to draw adverse comments. He accused the team of selling the club short and received this tart reply from some of the players, 'How does he know? We never see him.' One disillusioned fan described him as, 'A publicity hunter who dashes from the TV studios to the dressing room just in time to gee up the players.'

The break came through a sensational sacking. The FA fired

Sir Alf Ramsey, England's manager when they won the 1966 World Cup. They were hammered by the critics and public and, needing a famous replacement to quieten the storm, turned to Brian's old adversary, Don Revie of Leeds United. Then Manny Cussins, the Leeds chairman, decided (against the advice of Revie and the misgivings of some directors) on Brian as a replacement. Four of us – Brian, myself, Bamber and Cussins – met at Hove in July 1974, to thrash it out. Brian wanted to go; Bamber wanted £75,000 compensation. I leaned towards staying and reminded Brian, 'Don't forget that Brighton came for us when we were out of work and while everyone else was hedging. And that they have backed us all the way.'

Nothing had been pre-arranged between myself and the Brighton board, as Brian believed, but I felt the job was only half done and that we owed loyalty to Bamber for signing us under the shadow of a disciplinary commission. Not only that, but he had kept his promises: cash for transfers, no interference, accommodation in the best hotels and a new Mercedes coach for team travel. Brighton treated us wonderfully and I wasn't prepared to discard them even for the champions of England, but I could read Brian's ambitious mind. He saw himself jumping straight from the Third Division into the management of a European Cup side; he saw himself leading out Leeds United at Wembley in the following month's Charity Shield match against Liverpool.

He was bitter when I said, 'Count me out.' After nine years, the partnership was over. I stayed at Brighton, signing busily – so many players it's hard to remember all of them. There was Peter Ward, a striker, for £4,000 from Burton Albion. He progressed right through to Brighton's First Division team, won a place in an England squad, and has been valued at more than 100 times his original fee. There was Brian Horton from Port Vale, a natural captain who skippered Brighton from the Third to the First Division. He cost only £27,000 – anyone could have bought him and his wages were rock bottom. Football had given him a hard time. West Bromwich had cast him off as a kid; he had played non-league football for Hednesford in the Midlands; and yet, because of his determination and influence on other players, he ought to have been playing at the top level from the start.

I bought some good footballers for Brighton and Hove Albion but, as a manager on my own, I just failed them. In July 1976, two years after we split, I resigned and joined Brian at Nottingham Forest. I had stayed with Brighton for the right reasons and, in my opinion, I left them for the right reasons. A change is required at times and I think both of us needed one.

Mike Bamber had been wonderful to me. I could have anything – a new car, money for players, a salary increase. I took a long holiday in Majorca, then returned to resign. After keeping them clear of relegation in 1974–75 I had missed promotion in 1975–76 by losing an Easter match at Millwall; from that day, my doubts grew. I told Bamber, 'I'm going; I'm a failure,' and he said, 'If you call this failure, then I want more of it,' which was a nice note to leave on. Time has proved me right; Brighton, under my successor Alan Mullery, reached the First Division, while I, reunited with Brian, went on to greater triumphs: the League Championship, two League Cups and the European Cup.

The split showed us how we were both up against it without each other. Our strengths were divided. I dislike dealing with directors and sitting through long board meetings discussing plans for new stands; Brian does it like shelling peas. He is a genius on press relations, but he hasn't my knack for assessing, buying and selling players. As it happened, though, he missed me more than I missed him during those ill-fated forty-four days at Elland Road.

CHAPTER 12

FORTY-FOUR DAYS
AT ELLAND ROAD

The phone rang in the small hours. Brian was calling from Leeds and, as always, came straight to the point. 'Name your own price,' he said. 'You can have whatever you want to come up here and help me. It's too much for one.' I couldn't accept. It would have made a farce of my decision only three weeks earlier to stay and manage Brighton; but, because he sounded agitated and worried about the possibility of a conspiracy against him at Elland Road, I turned him down gently.

I must have been the only man in football unaware of the growing crisis at Leeds United. I had been so busy working on my own for the first time in nine years that I hadn't given a thought to Brian's problems. His call was the first contact between us since separating; after that brief conversation, I wasn't surprised by his sudden departure at the beginning of September 1974.

He lasted only forty-four days at Leeds United, and it's been calculated that his stay cost them £4,100 a day. The club balance sheet eventually revealed a payment of £135,201 to Brian and £45,000 in compensation and legal costs to Brighton. He also retained a Mercedes that went with the job. The figures boil down to £30,000 clear for Brian, which made him secure financially.

The money was some sort of cushion against the jolt of failure and against the bitterness he tasted while out of work for the next four months. Disaster must have caught him as unprepared as our early runaway success had; we shot to the top so fast at Derby that we didn't know half the people in the game and I suppose there was no shortage of managers waiting for us to fall. They didn't have to wait long once Brian decided to join Leeds.

He often talks about those forty-four days and believes the two of us could have overcome the difficulties of trying to run a club that he felt was ganged up against him. I think he made many right decisions at Leeds but was mistaken in trying to enforce them too hurriedly. Possibly, whatever he did would have been wrong, for the odds were stacked against him. He had lost friends at Brighton by leaving so abruptly to join a club where he had made enemies who were eager to pounce on his first false move.

The Leeds board was split and some directors spread the

impression that they hadn't known officially of his appointment. The back-room staff were uneasy because Brian had been their most severe critic; the players wanted their own teammate Johnny Giles as manager; the fans resented Brian's trenchant attacks on their team, and outgoing manager Don Revie did nothing to calm them. Instead, he went on TV and called Brian 'a daft choice'. It was obvious what lay in store for Brian when Revie's team appeared on the balcony of Leeds City Hall that summer with the League Championship trophy. The players were cheered by thousands of fans thronged below, but chairman Manny Cussins was heckled and every mention of Brian Clough was booed.

Brian tried to woo the dressing room with a telegram to skipper Billy Bremner saying, 'It's a privilege to manage Leeds United.' The gesture cut no ice. Some champion grumblers played for Leeds and they were quick to complain because Brian was still on holiday when they reported for pre-season training. Allan Clarke, the England striker, voiced the general opinion: 'Clough should be here, not sunning himself in Majorca.' Then, when Brian arrived at last, trainer-coach Les Cocker resigned to team up again with Revie as England's assistant manager.

Revie and Cocker left a side starting to grow old. Six players – Giles, Norman Hunter, Peter Lorimer, Paul Madeley, Terry Cooper and Paul Reaney – had qualified for testimonials.

These were granted as soon as possible after ten years' service and, thanks to thorough organisation, usually produced around £40,000 tax-free for the beneficiary.

Naturally, there would be anxiety about the risk of a new manager clearing out senior players before their testimonial seasons. Those fears must have increased when Brian offered goalkeeper David Harvey and defender Trevor Cherry to Leicester City in exchange for Peter Shilton, the 'keeper he always hoped to sign. The Shilton deal didn't go through, so Brian then made a signing that I would have vetoed. He paid £250,000 to Nottingham Forest for Duncan McKenzie, a forward whose fantastic skill is usually non-productive.

McKenzie is a nice, likeable lad but I would never buy him. He is the sort of footballer who ought to be on the halls; his ability is so individual that he is almost impossible to slot into a team plan. There seems to be a blockage in his mind which makes him retain the ball when it ought to be released; that's why he has shuttled around half a dozen clubs but has had only one outstanding season, when he scored twenty-six league goals for Forest just before Brian bought him.

John O'Hare and John McGovern, who had both slipped into Derby County's reserves, were also signed for £125,000 – two of Brian's old stalwarts and good players, but probably wrong for Leeds at that time, for the champions needed an injection of either super-players or, perhaps, none at all. It illustrated how Brian was experiencing similar difficulties to mine at Brighton, because the parting had divided our strengths; we were trying to cope with unfamiliar aspects of management. He wasn't accustomed to buying and selling, so he made mistakes and a crucial one united all his opponents. He tried to sell Terry Cooper.

An outsider like Brian couldn't have known of Cooper's special place in the affections of Leeds United. He was an entertaining, attacking left-back who played for England in the 1970 World Cup in Mexico. The terraces idolised him and he was extraordinarily popular inside the club, so there was general outrage when Brian arranged to sell him to Forest for £75,000. The board intervened. Chairman Cussins said, 'I want more information,' Brian was called before the directors, and Cooper stayed.

Brian's position was weakened most of all by bad results; the champions took only four points from their first six matches. A 1–1 home draw with Luton was booed and thousands walked out. Snipers were everywhere. Someone from the club staff was quoted anonymously as claiming, 'The new manager has forbidden mention of Don Revie's name.' An unnamed player alleged, 'We never see Clough and he tells us nothing.'

It must have been hell for Brian, who is among the world's worst losers; even a victory leaves him wrung out, his shirt soaked in sweat from sheer nervous tension. He has often asked me, 'How the hell did Busby, Shankly and Nicholson live so long under this strain? Every day I wonder how much longer I can take it. I go home, slump in a chair and start reading and rereading the league tables in the evening paper while watching the telly at the same time; I'll do that for a couple of hours and yet I'm not taking any of it in.'

The tide turned against him even at what seemed a perfect beginning – Wembley on a sunny August day with the stadium filled for the Charity Shield showpiece against Liverpool. Brian led out the champions to face the cup holders and no one foresaw the storm about to break when Bremner, the Leeds captain, exchanged punches with Kevin Keegan. They were sent off for this fight, which is disgrace enough at Wembley. But Bremner and Keegan worsened it by ripping off their shirts and running into the tunnel bare-chested. The FA, shocked and determined to set an example, fined each of them £500 and suspended them until the end of September.

Brian, of course, was blameless but the incident was an omen of the setbacks ahead. The match ended 1–1 but Liverpool then won the shield on penalties. The luck of Leeds didn't improve in the league; they beat only Birmingham City in their six league matches under Brian and lost to Stoke City, QPR and Manchester City.

A 1–1 draw in the League Cup at Huddersfield Town, bottom of the Third Division, was his last match, although the poor result in itself didn't doom him. His position became untenable just before the kick-off when the players said bluntly, 'We're not happy with your handling of the team,' and asked for Manny Cussins and director Sam Bolton, a vice-president of the Football League, to visit the dressing room and hear their case. Brian told me, 'Giles and Bremner seemed to be the main spokesmen, but I heard only the start of the argument because Sam Bolton asked me to leave, saying that discussion was being inhibited. Then I knew I could no longer manage the club.'

The news broke two days later with the announcement by the club of 'a mutual, agreeable arrangement to terminate the manager's employment'. However nicely wrapped up, it was still the sack. Brian believes he ought to have been allowed more time at Leeds and has often said to me, 'Fear spread through that club. The directors were frightened because I hadn't won the first seven games; the players were frightened of their age. It was the culmination of a thousand things – bad results, a few players who worshipped Revie and disliked me, a staff set in their ways. But mostly fear.'

He went back to Derby and turned almost into a recluse. I didn't hear a word from him, but I remembered the many times he said, 'Home is my sanctuary, the only sane place I have. And I'm going to keep it that way.' He changed his ex-directory phone number again and stayed mostly indoors.

Tony Waddington, manager of Stoke City, tempted Brian out of this self-imposed isolation with an invitation to be his guest at a UEFA Cup match in Holland against Ajax Amsterdam. It was a goalless draw, and the only football that Brian saw in seventeen weeks, until suddenly resurfacing as the new manager of Nottingham Forest in January 1975.

Contact with Forest was first established the previous summer on a village cricket ground at Widmerpool, where vice-chairman Stuart Dryden strolled round the boundary with Brian and they found they got on. This promenade didn't go unnoticed and Nottingham buzzed with rumours long before manager Allan Brown was sacked with Forest's team lying thirteenth in the Second Division table. Brown, a former Scotland international forward, nursed no grudge. He said later, 'I was the least surprised man when Brian got my job. He wasn't a party to it; they wanted him even before appointing me fourteen months earlier.'

Forest, the world's third oldest league club, were founded in 1865, three years after Notts County on the other side of the River Trent. A publicity-minded Victorian coined the club's name, claiming that their first ground at Forest Racecourse had been a clearing used as a hide-out by Robin Hood's merry men. The clearing turned out to be a backwater; nothing much happened at Forest. Sam Widdowson, their England forward, invented shin guards in 1874 and they won the FA Cup in 1898. It was their last major trophy for sixty-one years of promotion and relegation, until beating Luton Town in the 1959 FA Cup final with only ten men; their right winger, Roy Dwight, had broken his leg after scoring their first goal and substitutes were not permitted in those days.

So Forest were a name in football only for their unique administration; alone among the ninety-two league clubs, they were not a limited company. Forest had no directors; they were run by a nine-man committee elected by the club's 200 members. There was no waiting list for membership when Brian joined Forest. All the prospective applicants had melted away when the team were relegated from the First Division in 1972. Membership, though, was a bargain at that time; a couple of pounds a week secured a reserved seat, use of a private lounge and the exercise of a vote that gave the fan a real say in the running of his club.

A democratic club ought to have been successful, yet Forest weren't and Brian jabbed a finger into their basic trouble by saying on his first day, 'They reveal one of the English weaknesses, an inability to assess and keep good players. Every good player produced by Forest in the last six years has been sold. They got £1.25 million and the cash has gone.'

He sent again for trainer-coach Jimmy Gordon who, after

the Leeds fiasco, had dropped out of football and was working as a storeman for Rolls-Royce at Derby. He sacked coach John McSeveney and accepted the resignation of the assistant manager, veteran Bill Anderson. He signed John O'Hare and John McGovern for a third time, although for only half the £125,000 that he had paid for them at Leeds. And he began with a victory against all the odds and predictions – a 1–0 win in an FA Cup replay at Tottenham. The scorer was a reminder of how football is a small world and close-knit family; he was Neil Martin who, a decade earlier, had played in Brian's testimonial at Sunderland.

The Clough wagon seemed to be rolling again but became bogged down; the gates, after a spurt of fifty season tickets sold on his first day at Forest, stayed at an average of only 13,000 while the team finished just above the relegation zone at sixteenth in the table. Brian's second season, despite early exits in both the league and FA Cups, showed an improvement. Forest rose to eighth place but there was no increase in attendances and then, in the summer of 1976, I resigned from Brighton.

He jumped in with an offer and our show was back on the road, but the old arrogance had been tempered by a new realism; we meant every word when warning players, 'Produce the goods or you're out. It's our neck or yours in this business – and there's no way that we'll go before you.'

Brian and I knew the score even as Forest's ground filled and the streets of Nottingham overflowed for yet another parade by open-top bus. It was unspoken between us, 'We'll go when they decide that they've had enough of us. Whether the reasons are right or not, they'll get rid of us. The only certainty for football managers is that we all get the sack eventually.' That's what those forty-four days at Elland Road did to the Clough–Taylor partnership. They opened our eyes!

CHAPTER 13

REUNITED AT FOREST

John Robertson is the cleverest left-winger in Britain, yet almost my first words to him were, 'You're a disgrace and ought to be sent home.'

Forest were based at Augsburg for a pre-season tour of Bavaria; I had joined them in such a rush that the players met me for the first time in the departure lounge of Heathrow Airport. Brian had gone on holiday after outlining his requirements, 'The running of the club and the discipline are perfect now, but the playing side is dodgy and I want you to take stock of that.'

I had agreed salary, terms and title with Brian and confirmed them the following day with Forest's chairman, Brian Appleby, QC, and his vice-chairman Stuart Dryden. Only the three of us were in the ground and there was hardly a sound outside; Forest had no bustle of expectancy in those days. The two officials were always prominent in the campaign to capture Brian for Forest. Mr Dryden made the first contact at a cricket match and Mr Appleby approved the move because of his anxiety to modernise what he called 'the most unprogressive club in the country'.

The chairman had also urged Brian to renew the partnership with me, saying, 'You complement each other because of your unique, individual talents and besides, a club manager without a trusted partner can feel isolated when ranged against a chairman and seven or eight directors.' We discussed the team and my role at the club before Mr Appleby said, 'I'll be delighted if you can contribute towards getting us back into the First Division in three years.'

I went home to Brighton happy about starting work for a fair man, not someone trying to hustle me for success inside twelve months. It wasn't until studying Forest's team on tour that I understood the reason for the chairman's three-year estimate.

The itinerary was half a dozen matches against small German clubs; once we played against a village and changed in a converted cowshed. Munich was only an hour's drive away. Who could have imagined that in three years' time Nottingham Forest would play there in a European Cup final?

I ran the team for the first two matches and then Brian arrived from Majorca with his family. We took two taxis from Munich Airport, one for his wife and children and the other for ourselves; it was an opportunity to compare notes in private.

'They're nice lads and no trouble,' I reported, 'but that was a feat by you to finish eighth in the Second Division because some of them are only Third Division players, and there's one of them who had better make up his mind quickly about remaining a player of any kind.' Brian nodded; I hadn't needed to name anyone – once again we were on the same wavelength. A couple of days later we stood by a practice pitch watching an overweight midfielder-cum-outside-left perform what purported to be his warm-up for the tour's third fixture.

John Robertson didn't move out of a five-yard radius throughout the entire quarter of an hour. If the ball came to him, he slotted it back to the goalkeeper; if it didn't, he stood still. I said to Brian, 'Look how fat he is, it's scandalous,' but I shouted nothing to Robertson. My job was observing, not telling him what to do. I forbid coaches to yell instructions during trial games because that defeats the object of seeing what a player does naturally. What Robertson did naturally was loaf about!

He ought to have been withdrawn but we let him play in the match after promising ourselves, 'We'll sort this fellow out in the morning.' Brian and I avoid overlapping in talks to players; we decide in advance on the points we intend to make and in what order we'll make them, the arrangement being, 'You do your stuff, then throw it to me.' So Brian began with a chat about the previous night's match and then handed the players over to me for training, which I began by pointing to Robertson, 'You get back to the hotel. I'll see you there about half twelve.'

He was shaken and asked what he had done. 'It's what you haven't done,' I said, 'but we'll talk about that later. And it might save time if you start packing for home.' When I got back, he was by the indoor pool, a spare tyre bulging over his trunks. I sat down beside him. Brian had briefed me on his background: he was single, twenty-two, living in digs and had been fined by Forest in 1973 for lateness at training. 'He's been at the club since he was fifteen and has let himself become disillusioned,' said Brian. 'He thinks nobody cares about him and he dresses like a tramp.'

Even international recognition of his latent ability had turned into a joke when England manager Don Revie, unaware that Robertson is a Scot, invited him with eighty-four English players to a get-together in Manchester in 1974. 'This lad has stuck in my mind; I'm sorry he's not English,' said Revie, crossing him off the list.

Robertson, despite his defects, had similarly impressed me – 'Which is why', I explained by the poolside, 'I'm sitting here discussing how to save you from the knackers' yard, instead of bombing you straight out.

'I've joined this club to observe and, where necessary, to replace people, and I have a queue of lads for your position but I believe you could do the job better than any of them if you can give me the right answer to one question – not, "Do you really want to play for Forest?" but, "Do you even want to play professional football?"

'I know it's got "professional footballer" on your passport, but that's a phoney description. Everything is wrong about you as an athlete, starting with a spotty face. By the look of you, you must be birding it, boozing it and living out of a chip pan. Don't tell me you are plump by nature, I can see that for myself. I'm not talking about plumpness but about fatness. How can you expect to do yourself justice in such poor physical shape?'

Fatness was a symptom, not the cause, of Robertson's problems, which sprang from a couldn't-care-less attitude and a set of hangers-on who had found a footballer only too easily led astray. He was shaken and suggested, as I had hoped he would, the possibility of another chance. I couldn't show relief; instead, I laid down the law even more firmly.

'I want you on the scales this minute. You're to go on a diet and on extra training. I know about your associates, and you're to break with them. You're not a heavy drinker but I've seen you with a glass in your hand too often on this tour. So that's got to stop.

'You've fallen into the gutter, socially and professionally, and you must either climb out or vanish from the game. So you'll have to put your house in order immediately because there's no waiting time with me.'

Today, John must often feel like throttling me each time I phone him and start with a running gag, 'Is that your line crackling, or is there bacon sizzling in the background?' Yet that lunchtime lecture at Augsburg forged a bond between myself and John Robertson and, although I've been responsible for the outlay of millions of pounds, no deal pleased me more than launching the salvation of a brilliant player who cost nothing.

I was thrilled when the former England right-back Dave Clement said after playing against John, 'This boy is special and has to be marked very tight. Leave him alone and he'll tear you to pieces.' Brian and I were both delighted for John when Scotland picked him for their 1978 World Cup squad in Argentina. The news came only eighteen months after we had threatened him with the boot and fined him twice for being overweight.

The start of Robertson's rehabilitation was followed by the discovery of another star under our noses. No one at Forest rated Tony Woodcock; no one imagined that he would turn into an England striker and be sold to Cologne for £650,000 (then the German record fee) inside three years.

I had never heard of Woodcock when I arrived at Forest. He wasn't a name even in Nottingham. He was loaned out to Lincoln City and to Doncaster Rovers in the hope that either of these smaller clubs would take him off Forest's hands. 'Woodcock? He can't play,' was the general opinion and anyone could have signed him for £5,000. Lincoln City wouldn't even pay that token fee, because manager Graham Taylor believed that Forest would eventually let him go for nothing just to prune their wage bill.

My arrangement with Brian was, 'Don't sell or release a soul until I've seen them play,' and so I began assessing every player on the books as soon as I returned from the tour.

The reserves were playing against Kettering Town in a pre-season friendly and I went to watch them. Although Woodcock was not particularly on my mind, I asked John Sheridan, the reserve team coach, about him, explaining, 'We can get £5,000 for him, maybe a bit more. So I ought to make up my mind.' John said, 'Well, we have played him at left-back in the reserves, but he's usually in midfield, where he is today. He's not content in either spot, though. He wants to play up front.'

Sheridan didn't realise the significance of this remark, but I could have hugged him. The world is full of midfielders, only the rare ones yearn to be strikers. Woodcock's desire to be a forward meant that he ought not to go anywhere in a hurry, least of all for only £5,000. But Forest seemed eager to sell and I arranged for Brighton's chairman Mike Bamber to be informed. I supplied the recommendation, 'He can play a bit,' and suggested a fee of £14,000, double the highest bid.

Brighton ought to have signed him the same day but I'm glad they didn't. Mike Bamber didn't move with his usual swiftness and it was already too late when his first scout turned up. By then, I had seen Woodcock play up front. I noted his pace, his ability to turn defenders, his calm; when he was floored, he picked himself up and got on with the game. I like that.

Lincoln, who had been so confident about bagging Woodcock for nothing, now began to press us with firm offers. Every time Graham Taylor phoned with a bid, I advised Brian, 'Tell him the price has gone up by a further £5,000.' When it reached £50,000, the message was unmistakable – Woodcock was not for sale. By early November, only three months after my first sight of him, he was in the first team and scoring eleven of the goals that promoted us to the First Division.

There's no denying that the framework of the promotion team, as well as of the eventual Championship and European Cup teams, awaited me at Forest: namely, Viv Anderson,

Frank Clark, Colin Barrett, John McGovern, John Robertson, Ian Bowyer, John O'Hare, Tony Woodcock and Martin O'Neill; but the playing staff was also cluttered by dead wood. A dozen professionals were sold or released in my first season and five changes made from the previous season's team; we also tackled the need to improve the performances of Robertson and O'Neill.

The treatment for Robertson, as I've described, was a blunt, 'Shape up, or ship out!' O'Neill, withdrawn and often in the clouds, required time and patience from Brian and myself. Forest's view of O'Neill was a dismissive 'Martin thinks he's a better player than he is,' to which I retorted, 'That's not bad for a start, I prefer it to the other way round.'

I found, though, that Martin's faith in himself didn't extend to his stamina. It's a doubt not uncommon among intelligent footballers. He didn't believe he could last the pace in the dual role we demanded from him – out wide on the right as a midfielder-cum-winger. It took nearly a year to get through to him and, indeed, only the steady arrival of better players finally convinced him. Forest started winning and he wanted to be part of it; that brought the best out of him and ended his inconsistency.

The key signing that season, in September 1976, cost only £43,000. He was Peter Withe from Birmingham City, a 6ft 3in. centre-forward with a pedigree of reserve football and brief stays at tiny clubs like Southport, Barrow and Arcadia Shepherds in South Africa. I had arranged to buy him a year earlier from Wolves for Brighton after seeing him play and being assured that he trained keenly, lived right and caused no off-the-field problems.

Unfortunately, I couldn't sign him immediately for Brighton because he was away in America for the summer season and, while I waited, news of the deal leaked out and aroused the interest of Birmingham's manager Freddie Goodwin. He topped my £40,000 offer by £10,000 and Wolves accepted. I was angry on two counts: firstly, Withe had played on Goodwin's doorstep for two seasons without drawing a bid until I moved in; secondly, while aware of a manager's obligation to obtain the highest price for his club, I felt that Wolves manager Bill McGarry had let me down after confirming the transfer arrangements with Brighton's chairman Mike Bamber.

That was why I remembered Withe as soon as I saw Forest's central strikers; I knew he was superior. My homework on Withe showed he was the type who thrives on good delivery of crosses; I had had a high-class crosser at Brighton, an unknown winger called Gerry Fell who pinged them like bullets. I had imagined the damage Withe could do on the end of them.

Forest, though, had one of the world's greatest crossers in

Robertson and several other players – O'Neill, particularly – able to pinpoint their centres. Their service was tailor-made for Withe as his scoring record shows: sixteen league goals in Forest's promotion season and nineteen in the championship season. Then we amazed everyone by selling him to Newcastle United for £250,000.

Brian was always riding him. He rides everyone, of course, but I think he went to extremes with Peter, who was the most likeable lad on the staff. He once said, 'If Peter Withe drops back any further, he'll impede Peter Shilton.' When Withe scored four against Ipswich and asked for the match ball as a souvenir, Brian said publicly, 'He'll get no ball until he learns how to play with one.' It was a remark made for effect only because, in fact, the ball was duly autographed by the team and presented later to Withe.

Funnily enough, it was in the return match at Ipswich that I decided Withe ought to go. Everyone imagines that Brian sold him in a fit of pique after a dispute over wages, but that isn't so. His flow of goals was drying up; he scored only once in the last dozen league matches of our championship season, and I sensed that we might have had the best from him. Strikers often need a change of clubs to restore their zest and keep them ploughing into the bad places; I felt that could be the case with Peter. So I turned to Brian in the dug-out at Ipswich and said, 'Let's pull him off and sell him for the best offer.' Brian nodded and sent on substitute Frank Clark and, although no one guessed it, that was virtually the end of Withe's career at Forest. He played only five more first-team games for us. His last goal – again against Ipswich Town – was in the Charity Shield at Wembley in August 1978. He scored in our 5–0 victory and was sold shortly afterwards; a string of four goalless games in the next month showed how we struggled at first to play without him.

I have an old-fashioned idea about constructing successful football sides; I believe in strength down the middle – a good goalkeeper, a good centre-half, a good centre-forward. They are the spine of a side.

Withe, the big centre-forward, fitted my specification and then I looked around for a big centre-half. I soon found one in the reserves at Coventry City, but all my contacts advised me not to sign him. He was Larry Lloyd, formerly of Bristol Rovers, Liverpool and, occasionally, of England. We offered £55,000 and Coventry snatched our hands off in November 1976. My friends in football said, 'You're crackers. This fellow is the big "I am"; he's full of himself and no one can tell him anything.' I said, 'But on the other hand, he is big, he can head the ball, he is an international, he is tough and, besides, I like arrogant players. If he gets too cocky, Brian and I will sort him out.'

Well, I have to confess that Lloyd needed more than the

average sorting out. He was murder for the first few months; he seemed to imagine he was dealing with a pair of non-league managers and was quite undisciplined inside the club.

Interruptions from players are forbidden when either Brian or myself are speaking, but Lloyd cut in continually. He thought he had the right to say what he liked when he liked. We don't stand for that.

He argued with us from the start of the deal; he was very demanding over terms, the negotiations dragged on and the transfer almost fell through. He was troubled by a back injury but it was less of a problem than his big mouth. I told him, 'You want to keep your trap shut because we're the best thing that ever happened to you. We're going to win things for you, we might even get you back into the England side. But if you don't want to work for us, you can go home and drop out of the game because we're not frightened to write off £55,000.'

Lloyd made his debut for us at the beginning of December 1976 against Bristol Rovers. Two months later, Brian dropped him for disciplinary reasons after a match against Southampton. Lloyd had been booked for fouling Southampton's England forward Mike Channon. This took him, in an alarmingly short time, over the suspension limit of twenty penalty points. He had also engaged in a running feud with the former England forward Peter Osgood and admitted afterwards, 'I was lucky not to be sent off.'

Brian dropped him from the next match against Hereford United; that shook Larry, who offered to pay a fine instead. 'Accepting a fine would have been the easy way out,' said Brian, 'and that's not my way. Lloyd had to go, even if it damages our chances of promotion. Because, whether I am manager of Forest, England or Nottingham Pork Butchers I am determined to preserve my standards of team behaviour and discipline.'

I kept hammering away at Lloyd with the example of Roy McFarland as a person, a player and a perfect professional; but it was almost a year before Larry knuckled under. By then, we were back in the First Division and had lost 3–0 at Arsenal in September 1977. Frank Stapleton, Arsenal's centre-forward, headed a quick first goal while Lloyd was dozing at the back; at Monday's team talk, I criticised him in strong language.

Now, Lloyd is 6ft 2in. tall with a temper to match; he turned white and his fists clenched. Everyone saw him starting to rise from his chair, positioning himself to throw a punch. I stood my ground and warned, 'If you come for me, that's you finished. You'll never kick another ball here, or anywhere else.' For once, he saw sense and sat down and there was no more trouble for another two years; then he clashed with Brian in Athens over an instruction to wear a club blazer. It was the morning after our 2–1 win against AEK, the Greek champions, in the first leg of the second round of the European Cup.

We had been drinking and killing time until our bus to the airport arrived. When it did, we trooped aboard dressed like a serious, professional football team, not like a bunch of tourists. Sometimes we travel in casual clothes but, quite often, in club uniform, and the instructions on dress are issued in good time with no room for misunderstandings. So Brian was rightly annoyed on spotting Larry Lloyd as the only player in jeans and a sweatshirt.

'Where's your blazer?' he snapped.

'In my case,' said Larry defiantly.

'Go and put it on,' said Brian.

Lloyd refused. 'It's in the boot and too much trouble to get out.'

Now I don't believe that Brian really cared whether his centre-half wore a blazer or travelled in swimming trunks. The pair of them were aware that the principle at stake was obedience to a club rule and squashing insubordination. In any contest over who's the boss, there's no chance of Brian backing down.

'I'm fining you £50 for not wearing it,' he told Larry. 'Another £50 for not getting it out of your case. And every time you say no when I tell you to put on that blazer, that'll be another £50.'

It was like a game of brag; Larry kept refusing and Brian kept increasing the fine and they didn't stop until £500 was reached. As additional punishment, Brian dropped him from the next match and Larry retaliated by asking for a transfer. He withdrew the request later and peace reigned once more.

Clashes of temperament are always likely with Larry although, happily, curbed by the enjoyment of playing in a winning team. There is no cause for complaint while the trophies and bonuses keep rolling in.

Big Larry was an important part of that success. We won promotion to the First Division and the Anglo-Scottish Cup in his first season. The Anglo-Scottish, our first prize at Forest, was won on a 5–1 aggregate against Orient in the two-leg final in December 1976. Promotion, as happened with a couple of our triumphs at Derby, was clinched after our own programme had been completed.

We rocketed up the table on the run-in, taking eighteen points from the last dozen league matches. Bolton Wanderers were positioned to overhaul our total and would have done so if they hadn't lost their final home match against Wolverhampton Wanderers, a result that confirmed Wolves as Second Division champions with Chelsea as runners-up and ourselves as the third promoted team.

Brian was in Majorca with some of the players and had to phone the chairman's wife in Nottingham for the good news. I flew out to join him with the rest of the players on the following morning and we all celebrated this satisfying conclusion to our first season together at Forest. Yet, even while gazing round the circle of happy faces, the partnership telepathy buzzed with the notion, 'Now we'll really have to get out the cheque book.'

CHAPTER 14

BUYING FOR THE FIRST DIVISION

Kenny Burns was known along football's grapevine as the 'wild man of Birmingham City' – a fighting, hard-drinking gambler. He wanted a move but no club would touch him. He was a stone overweight. He had left his wife and children and was not on speaking terms with his club partner, Trevor Francis. He was at the dogs most nights, and that's where I went spying on him.

I trailed him between the bookies and the bars at the Perry Barr track in Birmingham. He didn't recognise me in my disguise of flat cap and dark glasses, nor did he realise that the punter so often at his shoulder as he placed a bet was Forest chief scout, Maurice Edwards. 'Tens and twenties, nothing higher,' Maurice reported on the size of Kenny's wagers. Moderate stuff, by my standards; his drinking was moderate, too.

I felt grateful towards the sportswriter who had pointed me in the direction of Burns. 'Kenny's not the bad person everyone makes him out to be,' said the reporter, a man whose opinion I respect. It was enough to make me investigate for myself instead of listening to gossip. I knew that Burns the footballer would be manageable. I didn't mind his excess poundage because weight can always be reduced, or his low boiling-point because temper can be curbed by fines, discipline and lectures. The hidden things bothered me, though – the size and frequency of his bets, the quantity of the booze. Happily, my night at the dogs satisfied me that his reputation had been blackened unjustly. I reported this to Brian and we offered £145,000, which Birmingham accepted gladly in July 1977.

Burns was our first signing to strengthen the team for the First Division. It surprised everyone, especially when we announced that, despite nineteen goals as a striker in the previous season for Birmingham, he would play for us as the sweeper. Perhaps it sounded insane to switch a goal-taker into defence, but there was good reason for our madness. I suspected that Burns didn't relish life up front; the running didn't suit his lazy nature. What's more, we desperately needed a sweeper alongside Larry Lloyd, and I visualised

Burns turning into a Scottish Bobby Moore, because he's as skilful as Moore and certainly more ruthless.

The happy ending was written the following May, and I'm not referring to the League Cup winner's medal, or the League Championship medal, or even to the place that Burns won in Scotland's World Cup squad going to Argentina. No, I'm thinking that Kenny Burns is the first footballer to lift himself from the dog track to the place of honour at the Café Royal in only ten months. For, in May 1978, he was voted Footballer of the Year by the Football Writers' Association and received his statuette – the premier individual award in the British game – at their annual packed-out dinner in London.

Forest had burned their fingers badly in the transfer market during the '60s with an ill-advised £100,000 plunge on a player who proved almost impossible to sell when they began trying to unload him. They suffered financially again in 1968 when the main stand burned down at a loss of £330,000. As a result, caution had become a habit in the committee room, but Brian and I knew that the time had come to spend, spend, spend.

We kept reminding the committee that match revenue would double in the First Division even if the team only plodded along in mid-table. We pointed to the forecast of £650,000 in takings and, on the strength of that, Forest's bankers raised their lending limit for transfers to £450,000.

We spent the lot by the middle of September while gleeful-ly assuring the committee, 'You have to speculate to accumu-late.' In activity, but not outlay, it reminded me of our days at Hartlepools, when we had once swept into Nottinghamshire and signed five players in one night at a pub in Ollerton. The £145,000 for Kenny Burns was followed by a new record fee for a goalkeeper – £275,000 for Peter Shilton of Stoke City. A few weeks later, we snapped up our old star Archie Gemmill for £20,000.

We cast our bread upon the waters and it came back but-tered. Every penny of those transfers was returned four-fold – with takings of £1,119,000 from all gates, £223,000 from winning the League Cup, £91,000 from reaching the sixth round of the FA Cup and £118,000 from commercial activi-ties, scarves and souvenirs.

Money cascades on successful teams and I am never loath to spend it. I don't quibble about fees; I would hate to lose a player for the sake of a bob or two. When we offer £250,000, as we did for Shilton in the summer of 1977, and are told that Stoke want £300,000 then my response is, 'Give it to them.'

Brian was as keen as myself to sign Shilton, saying, 'I long ago realised the futility of scoring goals at one end while let-ting them in at the other.' However, he is steadier with the cash than I am and so he refused to budge beyond £275,000. We discussed our offer with Stoke's manager George Eastham who warned us, 'Persuading your committee to break the record for a goalkeeper is only your first problem; they'll also have to break the record for wages. You must consider how to break it gently that Shilton is the highest-paid player in the Football League.'

It's no secret that Shilton's contract at Stoke was index-linked. He had signed from Leicester City for a reputed wage of £400 a week, far and away the fattest pay packet in British football. Now Stoke were relegated and their crowds were shrinking while raging inflation sent Shilton's salary to heights that scared the directors stiff.

I believe that a club wanting the best players must accommodate their pay demands, but I understand how directors and committees need wooing round to my view; so we worked a shade deviously this time, with Brian inviting the vice-chairman Stuart Dryden to accompany him to a mid-week match at Everton. They were hurrying out of their seats when Brian said, 'Let's go into the tea room first because I'd like you to meet Albert Henshall, the chairman of Stoke City.' 'But why?' asked Mr Dryden. Then Brian sprang it on him, 'Because we're going to sign Peter Shilton.'

The fee and the wages were the major part of our problem in swinging the Shilton deal, but we also had to counter the opinion in Nottingham, perhaps most strongly felt in the committee room, that we didn't need him. Forest fans believed they already had a star goalkeeper in John Middleton, an England Under-23 international. I drew on my own goalkeeping career to educate them into understanding why Shilton was infinitely superior to Middleton – and all other 'keepers, for that matter.

Signing Peter was one of the highlights of my career, for I had been obsessed with him since he was nineteen and already a fixture in Leicester City's first team. I travelled regularly from Derby to watch Shilton when he replaced the celebrated Gordon Banks, who had been England's goalkeeper in the World Cup win of 1966. The boy's maturity and technique were astonishing; he knew instinctively the tricks of a trade that normally demands a long apprenticeship. I admired his bravery, his handling and his temperament, but was impressed most of all by this teenager's mastery of positional play and marshalling defences – the arts that most 'keepers learn late.

Peter says he was influenced by Banks, by Lev Yashin of Russia and by Peter Bonetti of Chelsea. He explains, 'I tried to copy the positional sense of Banks, who was never caught moving as the ball was struck. I tried to copy the invincible presence of Yashin, and I tried to copy the agility and distribution of Bonetti, as well as his willingness to be responsible for crosses.'

Shilton's formula for the perfect 'keeper is: size, good

hands, agility, courage and personality. He has added dedication to those qualities, for I know how hard he works on refining technical details that the average fan may never notice – punching, for instance. Peter doesn't thump the ball haphazardly; he's aiming for the right height and distance. He is right-handed but spends hours practising left-arm punches so that opponents can never say, 'This fellow always clears with the same fist. If we crowd that arm, he'll be lost.'

The arrival of Shilton meant the displacement of Middleton, which was followed by events illustrating the importance of timing in the transfer market. Derby County needed a 'keeper in a hurry and realised that we might be prepared to sell Middleton; at the same time, they sacked manager Colin Murphy and brought in Tommy Docherty, former manager of Manchester United and Scotland. Scots often don't see eye to eye, and that was notably the case with Archie Gemmill and The Doc. He didn't fancy playing for the new manager and made his unrest public. We needed Archie's dynamism down the left of midfield and Docherty needed our surplus 'keeper. We offered Middleton and £20,000 for Gemmill, and it was accepted.

What an amazing deal! Gemmill figured prominently in all our success over the next two years; he won a place in Scotland's 1978 World Cup squad and, finally, made a handsome profit for Forest by moving to Birmingham for £150,000.

Poor Middleton, though, spent the same period fighting to keep his place while trying to save Derby from relegation.

Our last signing in that 1977–78 season came shortly before Christmas as another surprise for the vice-chairman. Brian rang Mr Dryden at his sub-post office in the village of Ruddington, asking, 'Can you come down to the ground in ten minutes? Larry Lloyd's broken a toe.' The reply was puzzled, 'I don't know what I can do about it. Surely you're not expecting me to play?' 'No! I've got David Needham here and we want to sign him.'

This £140,000 deal was sprung on the committee but they knew the player nearly as well as we did. Needham was a household name in Nottingham as a long-serving defender with Notts County. A few years earlier, I had toyed with the idea of signing him for Derby as cover for Roy McFarland. A close-season move to Queens Park Rangers hadn't worked out for Needham, who had become unsettled through continual travelling to London from his country cottage in Leicestershire. He wasn't the big-city type but a lover of the rural life who had bred horses and run a riding school. Our offer, giving QPR a quick £50,000 profit, suited everyone.

Needham was delighted to sign and his return created interest in Nottingham, although die-hard Forest supporters were dubious about accepting someone who had played for eleven seasons at Notts County. But we knew they would warm to him eventually as an honest, brave, cheerful footballer who fulfilled my first test of a player – the ability to pass the ball accurately when under pressure.

It sounds a simple requirement, yet a surprisingly high number of professional footballers cannot meet it. The capacity to knock the ball twenty yards or more to a teammate when under challenge tells me that I'm looking at a craftsman. There's a lot of emphasis on winning the ball but it's more important that the ball shouldn't be given away. At the top level, a man who can't pass can't play. The essence of football is the delivery, weighting, accuracy and timing of the pass. Ardiles, the Argentinian at Tottenham, is a model for youngsters in his precise release of the ball.

Some managers put pace as their number one requirement; for me, it's only a close second. I've seen footballers who move like lightning but produce nothing because they can't pass; and I've seen slow men make a good living through their ability to provide service on a plate. A man who can pass always has good control; the two go together. John Robertson is an example, for his control and passing are brilliant, yet his pace is nil. I like heart in players, although I would take a lad who hid from the nasty tackling if he could drop the ball wherever he fancied; but a team doesn't want too many like him. Temperament is crucial because sides cannot afford men who sulk or buckle. Brains, too, come into my assessments. If there are two lads with football ability but unequal intelligence, you can be sure that the boy with the higher IQ will progress further in the game.

I don't look for hard men because a flowing side can't be built on an overuse of muscle. Hard men stop matches by hurting people; their fouls can be costlier than bad passes, because a free kick gives the opposition unchallenged possession – and often in a dangerous area.

Brian and I have always sought to build sides that get on with the game. We want matches won in the right manner by consistent performers, not by thugs or fly-by-nights. Jock Stein, the Scotland manager, said in 1978, 'It's not just that Cloughie can gee up ordinary players, but he and Taylor know which fellows will go well together, will bring out the best in each other. That probably does more than anything to explain the fantastic record.'

The word on Jock's mind was 'blend', which we're always using in considering how to produce teams that win consistently. The difficult part of football management is keeping a side hungry for success and not allowing them to relax or lower their standards. Another major difficulty is maintaining the flow of talent from youth schemes. I cannot calculate the odds against a schoolboy-hopeful developing into a star, but my experience is that they are very high.

We watch boys play from the age of twelve; we take them

as apprentices when they leave school; we coach them and encourage them to continue their education through part-time studies. We know our boys are the cream from hundreds in their age group, yet it's still 20–1 against even this elite group producing a winner. There's no such thing as discovering schoolboy stars, they discover you. Anyone with minimal football knowledge could watch a boys' match and pick the outstanding player, but no one can foresee if he will progress or decline in his teenage years.

Steve Powell of Derby County often played two school matches a day, winning both of them on his own through his exceptional ability and physique. Obviously, that dominance couldn't continue once he entered the professional game and so Steve fell short of some people's expectations. He was in our first team at sixteen and I believed that Steve would play for England. In fact, he never went further than the Under-23 international side, nor did he blossom into a superstar. He found his level as one of the First Division's soundest utility players – and that's a success story when you remember the wonderful kids from thousands of schools who never get as far as a league reserve match.

The wastage of talent seems dreadful, yet also inevitable. I cannot see a solution. It seems to me that the game has been too easy for the overwhelming majority of schoolboy stars; they have strolled through matches from the age of eight, playing with and against inferior talents. They have never learned to stretch themselves, they have never been forced to compete. And so they have nothing to draw upon when they join a league club, where they need new ideas because they are no longer cock of the walk. Once the game becomes hard for them, they lose their zest. It's almost as though they are burned out.

Happily, there's always the hope of unearthing a late developer who survives rejection and beats the system. Garry Birtles is a classic case; inside two seasons, he rocketed from floor-laying to the First Division, from Long Eaton United to the European Cup. Long Eaton is eight miles from Nottingham, a non-league club with crowds that hardly ever number more than 400. There is no seating and the gents is a corrugated-iron enclosure beside a hedge.

Birtles, who had been on schoolboy forms at Notts County, earned a fiver a match as their centre-forward. My scouts never mentioned him as a prospect, obviously regarding him as just a run-of-the-mill part-timer. So I first heard of Garry Birtles in September 1976 when a friend rang from Burton, saying, 'There's a lad from Long Eaton who is going to Manchester United.' I was thunderstruck; I expect that sort of information from my staff. I phoned my scout for the area who said, 'Oh, Birtles. Used to be at Clifton as an amateur. Can't play.' I fumed, 'Whether he can play or not, if he goes

to Old Trafford and signs, you'll get the sack.' Then I phoned
back to my contact at Burton and asked him to watch Birtles,
who was there that afternoon with Long Eaton. He rang in
the evening, 'The United business is a bum steer. No one's in
for him but I think the boy has got something; he's no mug.'

The knowledge that United were not in the hunt took the
pressure off me; besides, at the time, we were more concerned
about results in the Second Division. The team were doing
badly and so, as we've done several times, I said to Brian, 'You
put your feet up on Saturday and I'll take them to Oldham on
my own.' Brian didn't fancy an afternoon hanging around the
house, though, and rang a scout who told him, 'Pete's sending
me to Enderby for another look at a lad from Long Eaton.' It
was a lovely afternoon and Brian decided, 'It's too nice to stay
in; I'll come with you.'

I didn't know Brian had been to the match until he trotted out that now celebrated line, 'I've seen Birtles – and the
Bovril was better than he was.' Yet I still felt the boy might
be worth a closer assessment and so I phoned Long Eaton's
chairman, saying, 'Look, you have no midweek fixtures and
I can't get to your Saturday games, so would you let Garry
come to Forest for a month's trial? Then if we sign him, we'll
give you £2,000.'

They jumped at the opportunity, because £2,000 meant a
fortune to Long Eaton. Our coaching staff found that Birtles

wasn't quite big or strong enough for a centre-forward and, not unexpectedly for a part-timer, lacked stamina. They played him in midfield and three weeks went by without even one hopeful report.

The reserves went to Coventry for a midweek match in the final week of his trial. Birtles was picked and I went along secretly. I took my wife and we paid to go in, sitting at the far side of the ground where no one from Forest might spot me, because I prefer to make my assessments alone without distraction. Birtles fumbled; he virtually fell over the ball. His performance only confirmed the gloomy reports and I ran through my list of checking points, telling myself, 'No. No. And No.' Then it happened! Birtles evaded a defender's challenge by dummying to go one way, dragging the ball back with the sole of his left foot and changing direction in an instant. He moved into the box, kept cool and shot. The ball flashed just outside the post. It was his only moment in the match, yet enough for me to decide, 'Yes, we'll sign him.'

I began to believe in the boy, although hardly anyone else did. I talked Brian into picking him for the first team, a league debut in March 1977 against Hull City at our ground. I went away on a scouting trip but returned to find Brian seething. 'Never do that to me again,' he said. 'The lad's neither good enough nor ready.' Yet we won the match 2–0.

Birtles waited more than a year for his next break. He

became disheartened and wondered about quitting football to return to his old job as a tile and carpet layer with his father. Six pre-season games without a goal in the summer of 1978 increased his misery; I fancied the boy but Ronnie Fenton, Forest's reserve coach, kept reporting that Garry's attitude was poor, that he was easily disheartened and not doing justice to his skill. I said, 'I can't understand this. I've seen Birtles, I know he is a good trainer and that his background is OK. Perhaps you'd better humiliate him, hit him. Irrespective of how he's playing, fetch him off in the next match. Get him off. Shame him.'

Fenton did as I suggested in the very next match against Sheffield Wednesday reserves. It worked wonders, yet Birtles was still only the second or third choice when a centre-forward vacancy was created by the sale of Peter Withe. Our first match without Withe was at Coventry in midweek and we sat around the hotel arguing through the afternoon about a replacement. I wanted Birtles but Brian voted for Steve Elliott and so, unusually for us, we turned to trainer Jimmy Gordon for an opinion. He came up with a third name, John O'Hare.

So Brian won the day and Elliott played, but within weeks Birtles forced his way into the team. He shot into the headlines by scoring the first goal, and creating the second, in our European Cup win against Liverpool, the holders and favourites. Birtles was there to stay and the following spring Elliott was sold to Preston North End for £90,000. By then, Birtles had scored twenty goals and was on his way to a European Cup winner's medal. We never imagined when selling Withe that Birtles would not only replace him, but outdo him. We were lucky, but what's wrong with being lucky?

CHAPTER 15

THE ENGLAND CAMP

Brian was interviewed for the managership of England in December 1977, when his rejection clouded a wonderful season. It was a blow for both of us because we were agreed that I would go into international football with him. The job had fallen vacant in the summer when Don Revie, after five matches without a win and successive Wembley defeats by Wales and Scotland, resigned without warning to become national manager of the United Arab Emirates.

The FA, taken by surprise, appointed a caretaker in Ron Greenwood, who was almost fifty-five and living on the south coast in semi-retirement after handing over the team management of West Ham United to his assistant, John Lyall, three years previously. Greenwood's England started with a goalless draw against Switzerland, followed by a 2–0 victory in Luxembourg. He then produced a result which, I feel, over-influenced the FA's selection committee. It was a 2–0 win at Wembley against Italy in a World Cup qualifying match which, although pleasing the supporters, didn't prevent Italy from going to Argentina as group winners.

However, Greenwood was in the driving seat when the selection committee met under the chairmanship of Professor Sir Harold Thompson, at sixty-eight only just the oldest of a panel whose average age was sixty-two. They interviewed Brian and Greenwood and four other candidates: Bobby Robson of Ipswich Town, Dave Sexton of Manchester United, Jack Charlton of Sheffield Wednesday and Lawrie McMenemy of Southampton.

Brian returned from London thrilled about his prospects and telling me, 'It went magnificently, I think we've got the job.' I didn't doubt him, knowing how he is rarely wrong in judging his own performance, so it was a shock when the FA confirmed Greenwood as full-time manager and fobbed us off with the joint managership of the England youth team which already had a paid part-time manager in Ken Burton. Three of us would be doing one job!

I agreed with the view that this appointment for us was reminiscent of President Lyndon B. Johnson's tactics in handing a plum American post to a political foe on the grounds that, 'It's better to have him inside the tent peeing out, than outside peeing in.' Brian and I could hardly criticise the running of England when we ourselves were part of the operation, nor could we reject the youth job because that could make us appear disloyal and jeopardise our chances should the senior managership fall vacant again.

We were both aware that youth football was hardly our scene; we are shouters and bawlers accustomed to handling senior professionals, not to treading lightly among sensitive teenagers. I knew the pitfalls in assessing seventeen-year-old footballers and how easy it is to be wrong. Indeed, Bob Hindmarch of Sunderland and John Lukic of Leeds United have established themselves in their clubs' first teams, and they were in an England youth squad on which my snap decision, hardly two years earlier, was, 'We've sixteen names here, but only one and a half players!' Clive Allen of QPR was also in the squad and he has been signed since by Arsenal for £1.25 million.

The offer to manage the youth team not only left us without an option, but placed us in a position where we could be made to appear negligent towards our duties. Within a few months, criticism from some FA councillors was being leaked to newspapers. A fortnight after our appointment in January 1978, we talked to the England youth squad at Crystal Palace but couldn't stay for their match because Forest were playing on the same night. It was a continual problem; our own team was so successful and engaged in such a surfeit of fixtures that we couldn't spare time for the youth side because their fixtures kept clashing with ours.

We resigned after a year but not before a bust-up with the FA at the Las Palmas tournament in the Canary Islands, where we saw for ourselves that some of the people responsible for the youth team didn't want us interfering in a nice little set-up of annual autumn breaks in the sunshine.

We wanted the team to be run our way and we wanted to win the tournament – which England did by beating Russia 1–0 with a goal from Mark Falco of Spurs. The celebrations afterwards, though, were remarkable for the coolness towards us by some members of the official party. Shortly afterwards Ken Burton resigned because he seemed to believe that he couldn't work with us, although there had been no clash because Ken isn't the type for showdowns.

All the friction was with the elderly FA councillors, the doctor, Professor Frank O'Gorman, who looked seventy but was hardly ever out of his tracksuit, and with John Bayliss, a member of the FA's paid administrative staff who has been touring with the youth team for twenty years.

Trouble started when someone ordered the team into the street to wait for a coach to the ground. We didn't want young players standing around in heat and traffic fumes before a match, so we marched them back into the hotel lounge, sat them down and began joking to relax them. The courier interrupted, telling us, 'Now the coach is ready.' We said, 'But we aren't,' and continued talking to the players. Ken Burton appeared next; his officials were seated in the coach and irritated by the delay. 'We're ready,' he said, so we spelled it out, 'We decide when this team is ready.'

Naturally, the atmosphere was chilly when the coach was boarded at last, and we had to wait only until half-time for the next bit of discord. The cause was the uninvited presence of the doctor and Mr Bayliss in the dressing room. We hadn't sent for the doctor because no one was injured, while the slicing of lemons, the self-appointed task of Mr Bayliss, ought to have been done earlier or outside. Brian asked them to leave, explaining, 'We never allow outsiders into dressing rooms because that's where we talk privately to players. Some important things are said at half-time.' They went under silent protest and I can't remember the doctor speaking to us throughout the rest of the trip.

The attitude was obvious; we were interlopers and boat-rockers and they didn't like us. I bet the offices at Lancaster Gate rang with applause when we resigned. I believe that a lot of FA councillors didn't want Clough and Taylor at any price and that's why we didn't get the England managership when we were better qualified than Ron Greenwood. He didn't win one League Championship, never mind two, in more than a dozen seasons of trying at West Ham. He won a couple of cups – the FA and the Cup Winners – in his early years but afterwards never extracted the full potential of his three World Cup players: Bobby Moore, Martin Peters and Geoff Hurst. His overall buying record was unimpressive, studded with so many mediocre players that I wonder about his judgement. Remember, a selector has to apply the same tests as a buyer!

Sir Harold Thompson, the FA's chairman, claims that success as a club manager is no guarantee of success as a national manager; but, despite the case of Revie, I disagree. The basics are the same: judgement, selection, blend and man management. In fact, it's easier for a national manager because he doesn't have the problem of persuading clubs to sell.

Ron Greenwood is a coach and it's a common failing of coaches to see in a player what isn't there, or to delude themselves into believing they can build qualities into players without the basic ingredient of class. Talking about set pieces and working to achieve marginal improvements in individual skill is vastly different from forming a correct opinion about a player. And the history of football is filled with coaches who have failed miserably as managers while making million-pound rickets in the transfer market.

Probably the majority of people in football were surprised by the appointment of Ron Greenwood, but he has handled England more successfully than anyone expected. He seems to have seen where he went wrong in the past and has not been too proud to delegate. A record of only two defeats in his first two years is hard to argue with. Yet I'm still not convinced.

For instance, Brian and myself would never have picked, as Ron did, six Liverpool players for an England team, especially when one of them – midfielder Ian Callaghan – was thirty-five and hadn't played international football since the 1966 World Cup. We would never arrange to play two goalkeepers in one match, as happened in Vienna in June 1979, when Ray Clemence swapped with Peter Shilton at half-time against Austria. We wouldn't pick goalkeepers on a rota, either. A decision would be made between Shilton and Clemence and, for me, there could only be one winner in that contest.

We wouldn't have carted around a veteran like Emlyn Hughes as a sort of non-playing captain. We would have started by building a younger side designed for the 1982 World Cup in Spain, rather than the 1980 European Champion-ship in Italy. We would have gone for youth because World Cup teams face a pressure game every three days and cannot afford old players who don't recover quickly from knocks and fatigue.

Above all, we would have gone for class. You win nothing without it, yet I think only four of Greenwood's squad through his first two years fulfilled the requirement of probably being a force in 1982 – the two goalkeepers, Trevor Francis and, because of his Continental experience, Kevin Keegan.

His defence would have given me nightmares – Phil Neal, Phil Thompson, Dave Watson and Mick Mills. The delivery from the centre-backs is poor (Thompson is the defender singled out for attack when Forest play Liverpool); Watson and Mills are too old and not good enough in 1980 so they have no part to play in Spain.

It's not my job to find answers for Ron Greenwood because I'm too busy watching players for Forest, but I'm entitled to an opinion about his side, especially as we usually provide three men for it. And I believe that Brian and myself would have put the emphasis on class, which means that Glenn Hoddle of Tottenham Hotspur wouldn't have waited two years for his first cap or been dropped after winning it.

Hoddle has youth, class and, as far as I know, the right character. I could throw him among the finest footballers on earth and be confident that he would perform at their level. The job of an England manager is to find another ten like him, not a set of good club men like Steve Coppell. Honest and hard-working, that's Coppell. But he hasn't got class. Ray Wilkins, his partner with England and Manchester United, is a negative footballer and nothing will change him. He plays too many square balls, lacks quickness off the mark and, although he can shoot spectacularly, doesn't score enough goals.

There's no escape from the test of class. Shilton has it, Francis has it and so does Hoddle. I don't see any fear in him when he has the ball. He doesn't get knocked off it; he goes through and delivers and he'll score more goals for England in one season than Wilkins will in five. Neither of them are in the team to score goals; their job is to create, but they both have powerful shots. Hoddle, though, will always get a goal when least expected; Wilkins won't.

Obviously, Ron Greenwood's interpretation of football differs vastly from mine. If it didn't, he would have awarded many more caps to Ray Kennedy of Liverpool. I rate Kennedy for temperament, for his reading of the game, for his knack of getting into the thick of the action and for the way he is always infiltrating by the far post. On the strictest view, he falls a shade short of the highest class, but he is able to play with the best and produce regular magic moments. I disagree with Greenwood's under-employment of Kennedy, nor can I agree that England's manager has been forced to stick with Watson because of a shortage of centre-halves.

I think the shortage was imaginary and caused by the fixed idea that the number five must be a big man. I'm confident of finding someone who is two inches shorter than Watson yet able to head as well as he can. I don't think it would be hard to find central defenders; there is someone playing at full-back or in midfield somewhere who would slot in. From Watson, an older player who ought to have been discarded two years ago, I'll move to two young players whose England prospects have been over-boosted – Peter Barnes of West Bromwich Albion and Kenny Sansom of Crystal Palace.

Barnes has tremendous pace and crosses a long ball, although not always accurately. His runs are mostly unproductive and, except by pushing the ball past and darting, he hasn't the craft to beat close marking. He can't put his foot on the ball and fool defenders. Some people believe that Sansom can establish himself as one of England's greatest left-backs, but I'm not among them because I've seen him taken to the cleaners too often. Fast men like Trevor Francis and Martin O'Neill turn him inside out. Physically, everything is against Sansom. He's the wrong shape (squat and heavy round the thighs), a clever ball player who'll need to wear a sweatsuit all his life and, although good in possession, not my idea of an England player.

Kevin Reeves, who was sold by Norwich City to Manchester City for £1 million in March 1980, is another for whom I see little international future. He is a predictable player, without the speed to escape from markers and not particularly powerful in the air. He is an honest player who is always making himself available in good positions and who will improve with experience – but he'll always lack star quality.

Cyrille Regis of West Bromwich Albion is more my idea

of an England striker. It's a pity that a cartilage operation interrupted his progress in the summer of 1979 because he, and Peter Ward of Brighton, ought to have been tried out long ago. Regis is still only a novice but is quick, strikes the ball firmly, has enough courage and can finish. I would have given him a chance, and Gordon Cowans of Aston Villa would have been capped early if Brian and I managed England. He fills all the requirements – young, unusually brave for a human matchstick and blessed with excellent control and passing. He is a top-class footballer who is strangely underrated.

Our England, then, would bear only a slight resemblance to Ron Greenwood's side; I think we would have arrived at a stronger selection faster than he did. We wouldn't waste time trying to develop players without flair or true class. There's no denying, I suppose, that our management would probably be less diplomatic than Ron's; we might find it harder to avoid disagreements with officialdom. Yet Brian and I are always confident of providing something that's guaranteed to calm troubled waters. It's called success.

CHAPTER 16

LEAGUE CHAMPIONSHIP AND LEAGUE CUP DOUBLE

Forest, founded in 1865, won the League Championship at last in May 1978. The Football League Cup had been won two months earlier and so Forest were the first club to achieve the double of league title and League Cup.

It's a rarity for a promoted team, especially one that came up only in third place, to scorch through the First Division to the championship. Since the war, I think only the push-and-run Spurs in 1950–51 and Ipswich Town, under Sir Alf Ramsey, in 1961–62 have come up from the Second Division and won the league title in their first season.

Yet I regard our success in the League Cup as the greater feat because of the handicaps imposed by injuries and the non-eligibility of Peter Shilton, David Needham and Archie Gemmill, who were cup-tied.

I know that the vast majority of managers would sacrifice their eye teeth to land a title, because that rewards consistency. Cups can be won by the merely lucky, the only requirements being favourable home pairings against undemanding opposition and a set of players able to produce their best in half a dozen matches, not in forty-two fixtures.

We were not blessed with such good fortune. Leeds United, the club who sacked Brian, were our semi-final opponents and then we had to face Liverpool, the European Cup holders, twice. The first match, the final at Wembley, finished 0–0, although as Brian said, 'We were shelled for ninety minutes.' We won the second meeting, a replay at Old Trafford, on a penalty. Five first-team players were not available for the game at Manchester, not only Shilton, Needham and Gemmill, but also Colin Barrett and John McGovern who were injured. I cannot remember a team ever winning a major competition against such odds. For instance, we fielded the youngest goalkeeper in Wembley history; Chris Woods, son of a Lincolnshire farmer, was only eighteen years and four months old. He had played only five first-team matches and was kept in the reserves for the three weeks before the final. 'We're in trouble if we have one player, most of all an eighteen-year-old goalkeeper, who thinks he's certain of a place at Wembley,' said Brian, sticking with Shilton as number one 'keeper for the league team and warning young Chris, 'Your only job is not to lose your place in the reserves.'

Woods had been thrust into the limelight by the non-availability of Shilton and the sale of John Middleton to Derby County. I knew, as an ex-'keeper myself, that the boy could do the job technically and I was fairly sure that his temperament was right. In fact, it was perfect.

Senior goalkeepers have sometimes buckled under the stress of Wembley, but Woods showed no sign of being overcome by the occasion. He faced Liverpool for two hours and was as unflappable at the end of extra time as he had been at the kick-off. He walked off with arms upraised while the terraces at the tunnel end chanted, 'Chris Woods! Chris Woods!'

There was a note of relief in the acclaim, because they had been two desperate hours for Forest. We had forced only one corner against Liverpool's dozen, while Woods had to save from Emlyn Hughes, Ray Kennedy, Jimmy Case and Terry McDermott. He was beaten once by McDermott, but the goal was disallowed for offside; he seemed certain to be beaten legitimately when a shot from Kennedy spun out of his arms towards Kenny Dalglish. The goal was open but Woods hurled himself to the right and parried Dalglish's shot for a corner.

Liverpool did the pressing again in the replay but lost after McDermott, controlling the ball with his arm, had another goal disallowed. They lost because of a mistake by referee Pat Partridge, one of those mistakes by which justice is often done. Phil Thompson, the England centre-back, fouled John O'Hare from behind in the fifty-third minute. Television replays showed that the trip was just outside Liverpool's penalty area, but the referee pointed to the penalty spot and John Robertson scored – the speed of his shot beating Ray Clemence's dive to the right.

'It was a professional foul,' said Thompson later. 'I knew O'Hare was a yard outside the area. That's what the lines are there for, and it was bloody unjust of the referee to give a penalty.' Mr Partridge, a FIFA referee and one of the most experienced British officials, was unabashed by the action replays and said, 'The cameras weren't in line with the incident. As far as I'm concerned, there was no doubt about the penalty.'

The FA, enraged by Thompson's frankness, charged him with 'conduct considered to be ungentlemanly, insulting, improper or likely to bring the game into disrepute'. He asked for a personal hearing and was fined £300.

The second sequel to our League Cup victory was the transfer at the end of the following season of Woods to Queens Park Rangers for £250,000. He had tasted the big-time and liked it. We knew he would knock on our door one day; we didn't want him to leave and yet we knew it was hardly fair to keep him in the reserves until Shilton retired. We offered

Woods more money but ambition was the greater incentive, so we couldn't hold him.

The League Championship was clinched only a month after the replay against Liverpool; a goalless draw at Coventry decided it although we still had four fixtures left. We won one and drew three of those final four matches and finished the season with a remarkable run of only one defeat in thirty-eight games – that was 2–0 by West Bromwich Albion in the sixth round of the FA Cup. We were unbeaten at home in any competition and unbeaten in the league from mid-November, when we had lost 1–0 at Leeds, to the end of the season.

Quite a few managers would be in a continual lather from the stress of fighting for success on three fronts – the Championship, the League Cup and the FA Cup – but our style of management is relaxed, allowing Brian to take a family holiday in February on the Costa del Sol. I knew he could go away for a complete break from football because his wife would hide the newspapers and I would hang up if he phoned for the results.

Mid-season holidays were pioneered by Brian; the innovation shocked traditionalists, who believed that a football club could only be run by workaholics doing a seven-day week from breakfast to midnight. Bill Nicholson, the deeply respected boss of the Spurs team that did the league and FA

Cup double in 1961, typified the over-devoted manager. He lived within walking distance of the Tottenham ground and spent every Sunday morning in his office. It was Nicholson who first set Brian thinking about holidays.

'He told me a story about his daughter's wedding,' said Brian. 'He saw her coming down the aisle and thought, "My God, she's grown up and for the past eighteen years I've hardly seen it happen." That's so sad I could have cried.'

Brian's interest in his family was not the only reason for going away at almost every half-term holiday; there was football logic in his absences, as he explained to me, 'As you know, what I give is enthusiasm and freshness. The breaks save me from going stale. I think staleness is inevitable without them because no manager can go into a dressing room twice a week for ten months on the trot and pretend he's bubbling over about the next match.'

Players can go stale, too. Three hours of hard work every day soon knocks the spark out of them. I remember the week before the second leg of our semi-final against Leeds United in the League Cup, when our routine must have been the least demanding in Britain. This was the schedule: Sunday, a day off; Monday, a stroll along the banks of the River Trent followed by a five-a-side match; Tuesday, a day off; Wednesday, a ten-minute jog and an afternoon in bed before the evening match; Thursday, a day off; Friday, another ten-minute run followed by a team-talk; Saturday, an afternoon match.

That wasn't a normal week, although I don't know if there is such a thing as a normal week; we tailor training to the circumstances. When a team is playing on Saturday, Wednesday and Saturday it is foolish to push the players physically on the intervening days, so we aim for mental preparation. Amazing good can come from walking and talking beside the river; when the weather is fine, we are better there than indoors at the tea room.

Yet it's a pity that Forest – unlike Liverpool, Everton and Manchester United – don't own a custom-built training ground. (In fact, we don't even own the main ground; it belongs to the council.) Our practice pitch is a squelchy stretch beside the Trent without shelter or fences; often we have to retrieve the ball from amid groups of anglers with tins of maggots.

The key to our fitness is the rigorous pre-season training; after that, a team expected to play sixty competitive matches a season needs only topping up. We wouldn't send our players lapping the ground while carrying sandbags or order them on midwinter cross-country marathons, and the proof of the pudding is on match days when no one can question our physical endeavour and staying power. Our system works;

that is its justification. The way that Brian and myself approach match days also works, yet our routines are completely opposite.

He'll lie in bed on Saturday mornings, reading the newspapers and eating a bacon sandwich. Then he'll drive to the ground with his sons, Nigel and Simon; perhaps he'll play squash before sending out for a fish and chips lunch for himself and the boys. Brian likes people around him before a match; I've known him to go to Antonio's, the Italian restaurant near the entrance to the ground, for lunch on Saturdays. He'll be talking to committee members, to his boys, to supporters, while I have a job to get him on his own. When he appears, he'll nearly always be carrying a drink for me, forgetting that I don't like alcohol before matches.

Sometimes I'll watch an under-18 match on Saturday mornings and then I crave isolation until the big kick-off. I stay in my office meditating. I go into a kind of trance – I've passed members of my family on Saturday afternoons without acknowledging them; the faces haven't registered.

We must be a complicated pair! You see, we reverse our roles after matches. He's the one who doesn't want to speak then and people often mistake his attitude for rudeness when really it's a release of tension. He wants to go home, and the better the performance the less he wishes to say. I'm the relaxed one after matches; I'm worn out but glad to chat.

I went from the dressing room to face the reporters, photographers and television after the draw at Coventry gave us the championship. I said, 'Ever since we signed Peter Shilton from Stoke last September I've said that anything was possible for this team because Shilton is the greatest goalkeeper in the world.' Shilton had demonstrated that for himself an hour earlier when knocking out a header from Coventry's bearded centre-forward Mick Ferguson, who said later, 'I was only four yards out and I felt sure it was a goal.'

Brian stayed in the dressing room swigging champagne from a paper cup. I told the press, 'Emotionally, he's on the floor,' but I suspect he was doing a bit of legend building that day, as the silent successor to Herbert Chapman, the only other manager (Huddersfield Town and Arsenal half a century earlier) to win the League Championship with two clubs.

There was laughter in the dressing room that afternoon and I was among the targets. The championship with four games to spare meant that I could no longer be urging, often before they've taken their shirts off, 'Now let's get switched on for Wednesday.'

I'm switched on myself throughout a season and find it difficult to relax; I wish I could ease off, instead of carting my anxieties home. Brian, though, can switch on and off. He's an organiser; his timing is good. He reads situations faster and often more clearly than I do; he knows when to put his arm round someone and when to boot them in the backside; he knows how to play scenes for maximum effect.

Only a born showman would have used Brian's approach to the problem of obscene chanting in October 1977. Television microphones were picking up the chants from the terraces; the words, filthy and usually abusive, were being transmitted into the homes of people who didn't often attend football matches and, after hearing the crowd's language, probably never would.

The game was receiving a national black eye and Brian decided to act. The Forest crowd were a long way from being the worst offenders but they were the ones we could reach. Brian ordered the painting of a notice board which was then placed in full view of the rowdiest terraces. His wording struck exactly the right note; no heavy condemnation, no pomposity, but simply, 'Gentlemen, no swearing, please – Brian'.

The Trent End chuckled and responded with cleaned-up versions: 'What the flipping heck was that?' when an opponent made a mistake and, 'The referee's a naughty' when decisions went against us.

There was a classic case of his human touch in January 1980. I sat in the office listening to him at his most persuasive when he was on the phone to a 47-year-old widow who was starving herself to death. Mrs Barbara Terry had shrunk to four and a half stone; she had refused the pleas of clergymen and doctors to start eating and had been taken to the Nottingham Hospice, a charity that aids incurables.

Brian, at the request of the hospice chairman, left a players' meeting to talk on the phone for half an hour and put himself over beautifully and effectively. Mrs Terry promised to end her fast and said afterwards, 'His voice reminded me of my dead father and he has given me the will to go on living. I have never felt such tenderness. Mr Clough is a truly wonderful man.'

Similarly, Brian did the right things after that historic draw at Coventry which sealed the 1977–78 League Championship for us. He didn't crow on TV; he wasn't photographed splashing out in nightclubs on magnums of champagne amid fragrant clouds of Romeo y Julietas (his favourite cigars until he stopped smoking). He said to me on the way back from Coventry, 'I'll celebrate tonight by removing my car from the drive and sitting at home with Barbara and the bairns.' Next morning he was up early, helping to sell the Sunday papers at his brother Gerry's shop in the Nottinghamshire village of Bramcote.

A dislike of fuss is something, in particular, that we have in common. Speeches, waiters and serviettes are not for us; for instance, neither of us attended the civic and county receptions in Nottingham the day after Forest won the European Cup in 1979. Brian was abroad on holiday, while I was trying to set up a transfer – but we probably wouldn't have gone even if clear of engagements.

We cherish a victory best by our own firesides, while parties, when we decide to have them, are restricted to ourselves, the training staff and players. We skipped the traditional League Cup banquet in London, preferring to bring the players straight home. Our championship celebration was held after the season ended, and in the most modest of venues – The Shack, a dilapidated restaurant-pub at Cala Millor in Majorca.

It's a little place you could pass without noticing, but the fish is always fresh and the proprietor and his family are pleasant and obliging. We get the drinks in, play cards, eat, talk, tell jokes, plan the future and put the world to rights. Colin Barrett always led the sing-song and Frank Clark was the star with country and western songs accompanied on his guitar. Those two apart, we were short of entertainers. We seem to have produced a serious team with no taste for frivolities. The season was over, the title was won and the leash was off – yet John McGovern and Peter Withe ran three miles every morning. 'Habit,' they said.

CHAPTER 17

EUROPEAN CUP AND
LEAGUE CUP DOUBLE

Alifetime dream came true in March 1979, when I led out
the team at Wembley for the League Cup final against
Southampton. Brian had sought permission for both of us to
lead the parade in the previous year's final against Liverpool,
but the league refused it. Our claim to be joint managers went
unheeded and Alan Hardaker, the league's director general,
said sourly, 'Things like this tend to snowball; the coach and
physiotherapist will want to go out next.'

Everyone knew of Brian's clashes with Hardaker and the
league management committee. He was contemptuous of
them and I felt there was a likelihood of him handing the
honour to me just to show the authorities what he thought of
their ruling. He didn't, though, nor did he ask me to lead out
the players when a second chance arose a few months later in

the 1978 Charity Shield, which we won 5–0 against Ipswich Town at Wembley.

I was so disappointed that I didn't go to the match; I couldn't face the indignity of bringing up the rear again. I went scouting instead and saw Bolton in an Anglo-Scottish Cup tie against Oldham Athletic. There were only 5,000 spectators and no goals, so that wasn't any fun, either. Brian's conscience eventually pricked him when we reached Wembley for the third time in twelve months, for the League Cup final, although he took long enough about asking me. I suspected he was set on a hat-trick until he suddenly asked, 'Will you take them out next week?' Would I? Why, as a youngster, I've stood among the crowds outside Wembley trying to buy a ticket at a quarter to three. I never imagined then a day when I'd march out first from the tunnel into the roar from 100,000 people.

We kept our intention secret so that no busybody at the league could intervene. I wasn't far from tears as the players lined up behind me, yet I also remember resenting the injustice of a regulation that forced Brian to the back this time. The two of us ought to have been allowed to step out side by side because it was our team; not his, nor mine.

I glanced towards the royal box, knowing that our families were seated somewhere in that area. Four sisters, two brothers and all their children and connections had travelled down for my great day; Brian's family was equally numerous. A whole coach had been reserved for them on Forest's special train to Wembley, the reservation notice saying simply, 'For the Cloughs and Taylors'.

My day was complete when we won 3–2 after being one down at half-time through a coolly taken goal by Southampton's left-back David Peach. The pitch was wet and tiring and cutting up from the start, so I believed we might outlast Southampton on it. Radio Nottingham interviewed us at half-time, something we have never allowed before and I forecast, 'We've weathered it and will take them in the second half.'

Garry Birtles made the prediction come true by scoring twice with left-foot shots. He was the first two-goal man in a League Cup final at Wembley for eight years, for the fixture had been earning a reputation for producing dull matches – but this match was good value, unlike the European Cup final two months later.

We wanted to turn it on against Malmö in Munich but we were a drained team. The players had taken too much out of themselves in a late run in the league when we beat Manchester City, Leeds United and West Bromwich Albion in succession to finish as runners-up to Liverpool, the champions. Even a break of a dozen days between our last league match and the final at Munich's Olympic Stadium wasn't enough to recharge the batteries, so our display was disappointing and Malmö showed little sign of wishing to raise the level of entertainment.

Malmö were coached by Bob Houghton, an Englishman, but their tactics reflected Swedish football at its most dour. Staffan Tapper, one of their few class players, went off after half an hour because of the pain from a toe broken in training; after his substitution, they concentrated on keeping the score down through the use of an offside trap. We beat them 1–0 seconds before half-time, when John Robertson escaped from three defenders and crossed a ball that Trevor Francis headed in; we nearly scored another on the hour when Robertson's shot hit a post.

Brian and I left the bench at the finish and crossed the pitch to the red and white end where at least 20,000 Forest supporters said through cheers, chants and banners what Brian put into a sentence at the press conference, 'It's staggering to consider what we have achieved in two years. We are worthy successors to Liverpool.' No one argued, even after such a dreary final, because they knew we had knocked out Liverpool in the first round and deserved our place at Munich on that performance alone.

The European Cup, when you think of Real Madrid, Ajax Amsterdam, Inter Milan and Bayern Munich, is easier to defend than to win once. Liverpool were favourites to hold it for a third successive year when they came to our ground for the first leg but, amazingly for a club who had campaigned continuously in Europe since 1965, they began pushing for an equaliser after Garry Birtles had scored for us. 'Because it was Forest, we began imagining that it was a league game in which we had to get a point,' said their England defender Phil Thompson. They pressed forward and a goal from Colin Barrett caught them on the break. He volleyed it in when Tony Woodcock headed down a cross from Birtles. Our clean sheet at Anfield, the finest performance in my time at Forest, sent Liverpool to their first defeat in two-leg football since 1974, when Ferencváros of Hungary beat them on an away goal in the European Cup Winners' Cup.

And I don't think any British club has equalled or surpassed our recovery against Cologne, the German champions, in the semi-finals. We had been two down to them at Nottingham – 'Dead and buried,' said Brian – but finished the match level at 3–3. Three away goals left the Germans with an enormous advantage and the bookies offering 4–1 against us, but I never lost faith. I backed us to win; I advised Forest fans to follow my example. 'Bite the bookies' hands off,' I told them.

Our 1–0 victory in the second leg came from a corner by Robertson, which Birtles flicked on with his head for Ian Bowyer, stooping to head the ball in. It's always diffi-cult to win abroad but we dominated the match and had a twenty-minute spell when we might have scored two or three more goals. The Germans blamed a first-half injury to their striker Dieter Müller, who had to be substituted, and said that 'flu diminished the form of their winger Roger van Gool, who has since signed for Coventry City.

I had plenty of time after the final to savour our successes against Liverpool and Cologne. The thought of them warmed me through a long, tedious night after the Malmö match. Our travel arrangements were altered because the Munich civic authorities banned night flights. We had to change hotels; the party had to split up, with the players in the city and the directors and wives exiled to Augsburg. How did I celebrate winning the European Cup? By spending more than an hour on the top deck of a German bus before going straight to bed. I didn't even have a drink.

CHAPTER 18

£1 MILLION

I sat up late at home worrying about Trevor Francis. I worried about the possibility of Coventry City beating us to his signature and about the risks being run in doubling the British record for a transfer fee.

It was already the second week of February 1979 and the deal had been dragging on since the New Year, with Jimmy Hill bidding against us for Coventry but not quite prepared to meet the valuation of £1 million. Brian was also trying to beat them down, but Birmingham City, the selling club, refused to lower their price, so negotiations were stuck.

Forest's committee had placed no restriction on us; our outlays were never questioned because success followed the deals, but Brian is the better businessman in our partnership and likes to save cash whereas I would go for the player at any cost. His approach keeps costs down but carries the danger of missing out. I thought the Francis deal was one of those cases because we were quibbling at the finish about a gap of about £75,000 in the respective valuations.

'This is ridiculous,' I told myself. 'We're arguing over bits and pieces.' So I went into my hall and phoned Jim Smith, the manager of Birmingham. 'Jimmy,' I said, 'You've got your million.' He replied, 'Thanks very much.' Next I phoned Brian and told him, 'We've got Francis; I've just paid their price.' He said, 'Good' – and put the phone down.

Two phone calls and fewer than two dozen words, that's how the first million-pound transfer was arranged. Indeed, the total cost was considerably more than £1 million because VAT, levies and the player's personal share of £48,750 added about £150,000 in extras. The deal doubled the previous record of £516,000 paid by West Bromwich Albion for David Mills, a forward or midfielder from Middlesbrough.

Francis had been recognised from boyhood as a well-behaved, outstanding footballer and so, unusually when vast sums change hands in the transfer market, there was little criticism of the deal. Nor, unlike our previous signing from Birmingham City, was there any need for a prior investigation round the greyhound tracks. He was the right age to go, at almost twenty-five, and even Birmingham fans, who would have had most cause to grumble, regarded his sale as inevitable.

I didn't expect major problems in re-teaming him with Kenny Burns, even though they hadn't been on speaking terms at St Andrews. Any resentment felt by Burns had surely been cured by his own success in winning a championship medal and being elected Footballer of the Year. Instead of being thrust into the shadows by 'Superboy' Francis, the achievements of Burns at Forest had left his old partner behind.

'Superboy' was the tag pinned on Francis in 1971 when, at the age of sixteen, he was a Second Division star with Birmingham and the youngest regular player in the Football League. Freddie Goodwin, then the club's manager, kept the boy's feet on the floor by making sure that Trevor escaped none of the chores performed by the other apprentice professionals. So Trevor laid out kit, scoured the dressing room baths, scraped mud off the senior players' boots and swept the terraces which resounded each Saturday with chants of 'Super, Super, Superboy'.

Goodwin inherited the boy from Birmingham's previous manager Stan Cullis, who signed him against competition from his old club, Wolves. Cullis delights in telling how he returned from a league meeting in London to watch a trial of thirty boys and, after only a few minutes' play, ordered his chief scout, 'Don't let that number ten out of here without signing. He's a natural.'

Everyone had been saying exactly that about Trevor Francis from the age of eight and everyone had wanted to sign him, but his father – Roy Francis, a former part-time wing-half at Plymouth Argyle – was too wise in football ways to allow any club to tie his son down on an associated schoolboy form.

George Best and Jimmy Greaves never won a schoolboy international cap; neither did Trevor, although he played in the final trial for England Boys. He trained in his holidays at Plymouth and at Bristol City but signed nothing, and was a free agent on leaving school. Apparently, everything had gone according to plan when he was earning £4,000 a year at seventeen and starring in a side winning promotion to the First Division; yet a basic mistake had been made in joining a club that manager Jim Smith was to call 'conditioned to losing'.

I watched Trevor regularly at Birmingham, noting the brilliance of his goals, his remarkable speed, his quickness on the turn and the way he left markers standing by hurtling through the space on either side of them. I always hoped he would become available for transfer – and that day came when Birmingham sank to the bottom of the First Division at Christmas 1978, as an odds-on bet for relegation.

Nottingham Forest had to sign Trevor Francis despite the flaw in him. I can best explain his failing by recalling a team meeting last season before a match against Manchester

United. I tried to rally the players by making them relive their hard times. I said, 'Just the word "Hartlepools" is enough to get me going again any time I'm in danger of sitting back. For you, Stan Bowles, it must be Crewe because that's where you were rock bottom. You, Garry Birtles, could easily find yourself back at Long Eaton United. And you, Kenny Burns, were going out of the game if we hadn't dragged you back.'

I was able to jab a finger into most of them, but not into Francis. It is different now since the Achilles tendon injury in May 1980 that threatened his career and removed him from the European Cup final and England's international squad. But, at that time, when I turned to him I could find nothing to say. He had never known what it was like to be a hungry fighter; everything had come too easily to him. Money had rolled in from all directions, particularly from America where he had a three-year agreement with Detroit Express.

It was the American connection that made the Francis deal so difficult to negotiate. Jimmy Hill had a tie-up with Detroit and was quite happy to let Trevor play for them during Coventry City's close season. We weren't. We didn't want him in America at all. We want players recharging in the summer months; we don't believe anyone can maintain form through a twelve-month season and we felt that a player costing £I million ought to reserve his efforts for us. If Brian and I had stuck to our convictions, Francis would never have signed for

Forest. We wanted him so badly that we were compelled to compromise.

We allowed him to play the 1979 summer for Detroit and all our worst misgivings were confirmed when he returned with a deep-seated groin injury and was unable to play for almost two months. What particularly annoyed us, though, was that he had been injured early in the American season and had kept turning out, trying to justify his fee of something like £5,000 a week. I hope Detroit hadn't regarded him as a commodity, useful to them only while he could somehow drag himself onto the field – but, unquestionably, the injury had reached a stage where he could hardly walk.

Trevor deadlocked with us over Detroit, yet in a most deferential way, addressing us as 'Mr Clough' and 'Mr Taylor' when talking terms and continually consulting a list of sensible questions compiled with the help of his wife. He was so polite and well-mannered that we almost moderated our usual lay-it-on-the-line and give-'em-hell approach to new signings. Almost, but not quite. We were buying Trevor for £1 million and for that sort of money we wanted the full potential that we knew he possessed, but which his career at Birmingham had failed to bring out.

Outstanding ability had won him the title of 'Superboy' without him ever living up to it on the field. His team had won nothing and Trevor was idolised for sometimes doing

little more than lend his presence to matches. He was dif-
fident by temperament and unused to harsh criticism, especially the Clough–Taylor brand. We had to balance the risk
of Trevor crumbling under our tongue-lashings against the
need to excavate the inner strength that we were sure he had.

Brian and I have been accused of being tyrannical but that
is not true. We are always guided by our knack of judging a
player's character, and that was how we handled Francis. It's
not outrageous, or a rule of fear, to tell a professional with
pride in himself, 'If you're a pound overweight or ten minutes
overdue for training, we shall want to know why. We have to
know everything.' I felt he needed something to put him on
his mettle, to keep him up to the mark. I wanted to impress
on him the necessity for always thinking about success. 'Show
us your medal, Trevor,' I jeered at one stage, knowing he was
empty-handed. 'If you sign for us, though, we'll absolutely
guarantee that you'll win something.'

Our promise was fulfilled inside four months when Trevor,
in his European Cup debut, scored the winning goal against
Malmö in the final at Munich. With a header, mark you! His
heading was something we tried to improve from the day he
signed. Brian began ridiculing the boy's habit of hunching his
shoulders. He urged him to stretch his neck. 'Explode,' we'd
shout. 'Get the rhythm right.'

I believed that Trevor had been misled by his own 'Superboy' publicity. Even as we returned with the European Cup, I criticised him, saying, 'One goal in one final doesn't make you a top-class footballer. You need a few more trophies and a regular place in the England team before you can think of yourself as established. Until then, you're a glamour boy who hasn't produced the goods.' They were harsh words, admittedly. But, as I've said before, Brian and I work through character and I remembered the comment by John Sillett, who had coached Trevor as a schoolboy, 'Deep down, he is a very strong character, able to stay level without getting tempted or big-headed.' It was something that we could work on.

When we wanted him to play wide, he objected, 'I'm better up front.' I said, 'Let Ron Greenwood pick you there, if he likes. Here, you'll play where we say. Besides, playing two roles will make you a better all-rounder.' He was afraid of letting us down and jibbed again, saying, 'I haven't the stamina to combine midfield and attack,' but in the end we convinced him, although he still prefers the job of plain striker. We kept trying to improve the deficiencies in his game, insisting, 'You've got to head it. You've got to chase back, you must challenge and win balls. We know all about your pace and the way you can lick markers and score goals, but you still won't justify the fee until you've ironed out your limitations.'

About a year after the signing, I had another dig at him in a team meeting. He drew me aside afterwards and said,

'You were trying to get a reaction from me, weren't you?' I said, 'Yes, that's the object of all discussions here – but I didn't get one.' He retorted, 'No, and you're not going to.' I sighed. 'Look, Trevor, when we bought you we paid a million for a man in a relegation team who was on the injured list and had won nothing in his life. What's the transformation now? You're becoming a regular with England, you've won a European Cup medal and a Super Cup medal and you're going to Wembley for our third League Cup final. Would you have done all that if we hadn't driven you so hard?' He had to confess, 'No.'

Both of us, Brian and myself, are aware that Trevor will always revert to his casual ways, but he is aware now that we will never flinch from our duty to bring him up to scratch. He must have known that long before he signed for us, because Brian had pulled him up before a television audience during the screening of ATV's Midlands Soccer Awards in Birmingham. Trevor mounted the rostrum only to have his prize withheld momentarily by Brian, who, instead of making the presentation, said, 'You'll get nothing here until you take your hands out of your pockets.'

He made his debut for us one Saturday morning in an 'A' team match against Notts County; the crowd numbered about forty. He had been out injured for some time and we were eager to see him in action, but we hustled him in too quickly and committed a technical offence. So there was an extra £250 on the fee for Trevor Francis; that was the amount of our fine for playing him before the transfer had been registered by the FA.

We had nearly signed Charlie George from Derby County two months before the deal for Francis. A fee was agreed, but the Derby board overruled manager Tommy Docherty. The directors pointed out that Charlie was being released only because of an expressed desire to return to the south and, of course, Forest didn't fit that bill. Brian called the Derby board 'horse dealers' and they reported him to the league, although nothing came of it. Charlie, meanwhile, was sold to Southampton for £350,000, but could have joined us if he had stuck to his guns; I don't believe that a court of law would have upheld Derby's action in telling a transfer-listed player where he couldn't go.

I watched two foreign players in the same season, Rudi Geels and Rainer Bonhof, a Dutchman and a German. Brian watched Geels with me and we agreed that, although a natural scorer, he was too old to compete against First Division defenders. Bonhof was crossed off the list, too. He was magical at free kicks, but I didn't see him wanting to win the ball, I didn't see him delivering it and I didn't see enough mobility. A foreigner entering English football needs a sharp edge. If he isn't willing to battle, he'll be swept aside – unless he is gifted to the eyeballs.

So we didn't buy George, we didn't buy Geels or Bonhof. Our only signing of the 1978–79 season was Trevor Francis, which made him one of three famous firsts for Forest that season.

We were the first club to win the League Cup in successive years and the first club to bring the European Cup to the Midlands. But, perhaps, we'll be remembered longest as the first British club to pay £1 million for a player. Like Sir Roger Bannister with the first four-minute mile, that's the tag which Trevor Francis can never lose – the medal we've pinned on him for life.

CHAPTER 19

PLAYING THE
TRANSFER MARKET

S outhend on a Friday night was the scene of my guilty
secret, the reason I smile wryly whenever sports writers over-praise me as 'the star-finder who always gets it
right'. The transfer market is full of pitfalls and no one in
it is infallible. We've all made mistakes in buying, selling or
talent spotting and time has shown that my biggest was in
August 1969.

Brian was with me, the resort was packed and the only
beds we could find were in a drab boarding house; the player
we'd gone to watch didn't have a kick and his team, Scunthor-
pe United, lost 3–0. He was valued at only £15,000 but didn't
look worth it that night. He was too small, he didn't know
where to run or wait and he hadn't the physique or experience
for his job of playing alone up front. I ought to have realised

that his best position would be striking from midfield or from just behind the front runners; instead, I crossed him off my list.

Two years went by before I heard of him again. He had gone up in the world, fetching a £30,000 fee and joining Liverpool. His name was Kevin Keegan.

I made another mistake in the summer of 1979 when signing Asa Hartford from Manchester City for £450,000. We had sold Archie Gemmill to Birmingham City and needed a younger replacement of similar style. Asa Hartford, a Scottish international like Gemmill, seemed ideal. He was competitive and ruthless, but I hadn't absorbed the full implications of the comment by Manchester City manager Malcolm Allison that 'Asa only lends you the ball'. We wanted a midfielder with vision but found that Asa, in the playing sense, wore blinkers. He couldn't see further than twenty yards; his passes were accurate but far too short.

I've heard rumours of contractual arguments between Forest and Asa after the signing, but they are not true. He toed the line, he was a likeable lad and tried his best, but he couldn't give us a change of direction, the switch of play from left to right that we needed because defences were beginning to read John Robertson. A mistake in the market, whether for a tenner or £450,000, keeps me awake worrying about an answer. I couldn't sleep over Asa until remembering that

Everton had been prominent contenders for his signature. I knew that Gordon Lee, their manager, was as straight as a die and would not shilly-shally over any proposition put to him.

I phoned Lee one night, explaining that Asa didn't fit our system and that a move was possible. 'Are you still interested?' I asked. He said he was, so we arranged a midweek meeting at a hotel near Blackburn where Forest were preparing for a League Cup tie. The players were going to their rooms after lunch but I said, 'Not you, Asa. There's someone I'd like you to meet.' It was a blazing August afternoon and we walked on the lawn where, just as I was breaking the news about Everton, Gordon Lee appeared and completed the signing without a hitch.

We recouped most of our money through the sale to Everton, losing not much more than the VAT on our original transaction with Manchester City. A small loss is always preferable to trying to justify an unsuccessful signing, although never before had a big-fee international of Asa Hartford's status been shuttled in and out of a club inside two months.

Asa was staggered when Gordon Lee walked towards him, and so I smile at Asa's later claims that he was glad to escape from Forest's rule of fear. He said, 'Even relaxing round a lunch table, players were terrified of saying anything that might upset Brian Clough. No one knew what mood he was going to be in; he liked to keep people on edge. Sometimes he would turn up half an hour late for a team talk, exclaiming, "Oh, there you are," as though he'd been the one kept waiting.' Hartford also complained, 'Clough doesn't like players having opinions. Once, after chipping a ball to John Robertson, he drawled to me, "We don't chip balls here, we drive them." I started to explain but caught Kenny Burns signalling me to shut up.'

It's true that Brian is unpredictable; no one knows that better than myself. And no one has put it better than Archie Gemmill: 'A player can never feel too sure himself with Clough. That's his secret.' If we ruled by fear, would Gemmill have signed for us twice? Or John O'Hare and John McGovern? They have played for Brian at four clubs. Harry Storer's favourite boast was, 'I've never had a player who has refused to join me again.' We can echo that. Hartford wasn't with us long enough to understand how we work; he was a mistake which we corrected swiftly.

Maybe I made a mistake at Derby County by refusing to pay £90,000 to Carlisle United for Stan Bowles. Eight years later, in December 1979, I brought him to Forest from QPR for £250,000. Everyone recognised Stan's playing qualities but, like myself, were alarmed by his reputation as an incurable, heavy gambler. He was usually broke and, in those early days, often unreliable and unpunctual. Manchester City and Bury had sacked him and he was reduced, in September 1970, to borrowing 30p for a single rail ticket to Crewe for a last-chance interview. Manager Ernie Tagg won Stan over immediately by saying, 'I've heard you're hard up, son, so here's a tenner whether you sign or not.'

Some of Crewe's staunchest fans still swear that 'Stan Bowles was the finest footballer we've ever had', but he didn't stay long. Carlisle bought him for £12,000 and sold him for £110,000 to QPR in 1972. He played for England, then walked out of the international squad in a huff and was discovered at the White City dog stadium in London. He was forgiven eventually and recalled to the England team. Sensational headlines and confessions marked his seven years at QPR. He did the lot – gambling, walk-outs, transfer requests, domestic splits, reconciliations and, finally, divorce. Yet criticism was rarely directed at his football; it was conceded that Stan could play.

I knew he was an enthusiastic trainer and figured that, at thirty, he might be maturing as a person. I thought the left side of our midfield needed someone with his ball control, so we tried for him. The deal was done through QPR's chairman Jim Gregory because the manager, Tommy Docherty, was in hospital after being punched and kicked by a gang of Manchester City fans. Stan's inside story of the transfer made us laugh in the dressing room on the night we played Dynamo Berlin at Nottingham in the European Cup. He said, 'Jim

Gregory phoned asking me if I'd like a move and I said, "Not particularly, because you've promised me a testimonial in 1981." He said, "You might fancy it when I tell you who it is." So I said, "Let me guess – Spurs or another London club." He said, "No, it's Big-head and his mate," so I said very quickly, "In that case, I'd better go and see them.'" Stan was tying his boots when I asked, 'You knew who he meant, then?' Quite unabashed, he said, 'Yes, Brian and you.'

The Bowles signing also provided a laugh at the expense of Forest's chairman, Stuart Dryden, who had been asked to call at the office but not told why. He entered and began to apologise, 'Sorry, I didn't know that someone was with you.' Brian twinkled, 'Chairman, you'd better come in and meet Stan Bowles because you're just about to sign him.'

Stan scored with a header, from a cross by Garry Birtles, in his first home game. It was against Aston Villa and ended a worrying run of two months without a league win. He was thrilled to play in the Super Cup, an annual fixture between the respective holders of the European Cup and the Cup Winners' Cup. We beat Barcelona 2–1 over the two legs and Stan said, 'Do you know this is my first medal since I was a kid in the Manchester Sunday League? I've had England caps under Sir Alf Ramsey, Joe Mercer and Don Revie but I've won nothing with a club. That's why I joined you.'

Complacency often sets in when clubs win honours;

managers sit back, satisfied with their side. That's not our way, though. I followed our victory in the European Cup by the quick signings of Asa Hartford and then Frank Gray from Leeds United. I've no regrets about signing Frank, although the move for him was in response to a crisis at left-back. Colin Barrett, our first choice for the position at number three, had missed most of the season through injury and the forecasts about his recovery were not encouraging. Then Frank Clark, the dependable veteran who had deputised in the European Cup final and was counted on for a further season, retired suddenly to become assistant manager of Sunderland.

Brian was in Majorca on holiday; it was already mid-July and I had to move quickly because left-backs are scarce. I read my notes and reduced the possibilities to Steve Buckley of Derby County and Gray, but I decided against trying for Buckley because of the risk that Derby would block the transfer as they had done with Charlie George. I phoned Jimmy Adamson, the manager of Leeds, asking bluntly, 'Is Frank Gray available? I want no messing, yes or no?' He replied, 'Yes, if the price is right.'

Adamson and Dave Blakey, his chief scout, met me on the M1 and asked for half a million; I offered £300,000 and we split the difference. The deal was done in a day because Frank was keen to join a team of winners, although he had been shocked to learn that Leeds, his club since schooldays, were prepared to sell him. Adamson, who had just bought the Blackburn Rovers right-back Kevin Hird, apparently feared that a pairing of Hird and Gray would mean that Leeds had non-tackling full-backs.

My signing of Gray has been criticised on the same grounds, and it's true that Frank is not a ball winner, but he has pace, a good left foot and the skill that comes from starting as a winger. And, as I must stress, left-backs are scarce. Frank fits into a side that goes forward like Forest; with Peter Shilton in goal and Larry Lloyd and Kenny Burns as central defenders, we can afford the luxury of two attacking full-backs in Gray and Viv Anderson. It's a question of blend.

I had blend on my mind when agreeing to sign Peter Ward from Brighton. This was to replace Tony Woodcock, who had moved to Cologne for £650,000, although Tottenham Hotspur were prepared to pay £1 million. We advised Woodcock of Tottenham's interest, but he shook his head. We offered him a big pay rise and a three-year contract to stay, but he didn't want that, either. His heart was no longer in Forest; he was determined to play abroad and in November 1979 we let him go.

I believe that Shilton could have been lost to a foreign club, too, if his pay had not been raised to a figure generally reported at £1,200 a week. Forest's committee didn't want to pay up; their dilemma was put neatly by one of the members,

'We can't afford to pay him, but we can't afford to lose him.' Brian and I have initiated the building of two new stands – the Ley Stand at Derby and the Executive Stand at Nottingham – but we have never forgotten that the first priority of a football club is its team. Shilton is a world-class player and deserves to be paid accordingly as the way to retain him.

I hope Peter stays at Forest as long as I do, and I wish the other Peter (Ward of Brighton) had signed for us last season. I saw Ward slotting straight into Woodcock's position, with Trevor Francis striking from midfield; everything about the deal looked right, yet everything went wrong.

I had signed Ward for Brighton from Burton Albion for £4,000 – a deal that came about through appointing Ken Gutteridge, Burton's manager, as a coach at Brighton. He told me, 'I've two or three players at Burton who are good enough for the Third Division. They are Ward, Corrigan and Pollard. Clubs have looked but turned them down. Now will you have a look?' I sent my assistant manager Brian Daykin, who watched them in an away match and gave the thumbs down. Gutteridge, though, persisted and said, 'You must rate me to have fetched me all the way from Burton to Brighton so at least give me the satisfaction of seeing these three for yourself.'

There was no answer to that, so I went to Burton and watched them in the second leg of the FA Trophy semi-final against Matlock Town, whose centre-half was Peter Swan, the old England player. Swan gave Ward a hard time and Burton lost, but I still thought, 'Yes, he'll do.' Burton played at Maidstone four days later and I took Brian Daykin with me. He'd seen Ward once and voted no, and I'd seen him once and voted yes, so it seemed a good idea to watch him together. The pitch was bad; Burton, who had turned up with a scratch side, were bad; and Ward was bad – yet he still showed a few class touches, enough to make him worth a £4,000 gamble.

Ward has scored a hat-trick for England Under-21s and had a place in the full England squad, but I don't think he'll realise his full potential because of inconsistency. Yet I like him. He is very good with his back to goal, because he can turn and lick defenders and finish. That's the rare quality – sticking it in the net.

I thought he would be good value for Forest at £300,000, the price I agreed with Brighton chairman Mike Bamber on the night before leaving for a European Cup tie in Romania. The signing was arranged for the day after our return but, shortly after landing, I heard a story that Derby County were hoping to exchange Gerry Daly, their Irish midfield player, for Ward. Efforts to contact Alan Mullery, Brighton's manager, were unsuccessful, which made me suspicious. Then Brian, for the first time in our partnership, doubted my judgement and asked, 'Are you right about Ward?'

I felt floored and insulted. 'Right?' I shouted. 'I've got every detail about him except his fingerprints. I've bought him once; I've played him. He's tried and tested. I know him as well as I know you' – and, with that, I left the ground. Brian, on seeing my conviction and eagerness to complete the deal, then got in touch himself with Mullery and Bamber but found them no longer anxious to sell, because Ward was returning to form. He played at Forest in November and gave a dazzling display in Brighton's 1–0 win. This was our first home defeat in the league for fifty-one consecutive matches, stretching back to April 1977. Mullery said afterwards, 'You couldn't have him now for £600,000.'

Another deal that failed that season was the loan transfer of Charlie George from Southampton in January 1980. I've fancied Charlie since he was eighteen and already in Arsenal's first team. His distribution was inspired, he was a reasonable finisher and I thought he was certain of a long run in the England team. Indeed, it's still hard to believe that he won only one cap.

We had a tip-off at Derby that he might be available, so we rang Bertie Mee, Arsenal's manager, immediately. He got out of bed to tell us, 'No.' Some years later Dave Mackay signed him for Derby and, a couple of years ago, the board at Derby kiboshed his transfer to Forest. So Charlie was nearly thirty before we finally got our hands on him. Southampton were on a winning run without him, so I asked their manager, Lawrie McMenemy, 'What's the position?' McMenemy agreed, 'Of course, you can have a month's look at his fitness because he is fit, even though he's been off for virtually a year.' We settled on £500,000 if a permanent transfer was confirmed, although I felt that figure was negotiable.

Bad weather restricted Charlie to three matches in his month, two of them in the Super Cup, so we asked him to stay for a further month. He refused, and has said since that he was homesick. He didn't give us that reason but said bluntly, 'I've been here long enough. Make your mind up.' I told him, 'In that case, it's no,' and then he surprised me by asking to play against Bristol City the following day, the last of his loan period. It was a mistake, because he didn't have a kick and on Sunday, when he phoned me saying that he had reconsidered and would like to stay another month, I had to say, 'Sorry, you're too late now.'

Charlie's a lively character and we all enjoyed every minute of his stay, but always at the back of our minds was the report of our medical staff: 'He's got a footballer's knee, a slight touch of arthritis. It's no worse than many play with all their lives, but it's not a £500,000 knee – or anything like it.' If he had stayed when we first asked, it's possible that we might have started renegotiating with Southampton at a vastly reduced figure – but that last game killed our interest.

CHAPTER 20

CLASS PLAYERS

Liverpool will understand that it's a genuine compliment, not an illegal approach, to say that Kenny Dalglish is the perfect player that Brian and I dream of signing.

Dalglish is the first name a manager writes on the team sheet. He's a player who never cheats; he wouldn't know how. He's the one always plugging away at the sharp end where the boots are flying; the one who gets up immediately when knocked down and who doesn't retaliate. He's the one who looks you in the eye, who offers a solid handshake, who doesn't flinch from playing a lone hand against four angry men, the one who runs until he drops. And the one who is never absent injured.

It puzzles me that he played so many splendid seasons with Celtic but never won the ballot for Scotland's Footballer of the Year. The English football writers elected him after only two seasons; I won't say that they are necessarily better judges but only that Dalglish joined a better side. He couldn't have fitted more smoothly into the Liverpool team if Bob Paisley had designed him; his skill, involvement and mobility remind me of Ian St John, the model for Anfield strikers.

I think that Kenny Dalglish represents everything good in English football and I criticise him only for not scoring even more goals. An average of just over twenty goals a season would be heaven sent for most clubs, but is not enough in a side with Liverpool's class and attacking style.

After Dalglish, I would sign Liam Brady from Arsenal. If class is the ability to put the ball where you want, then he oozes it. This little Irishman is the tops for vision and accuracy and, what's more, I don't think we've seen the best of him yet. And I think he ought to stop drifting into his own back four; his job is staying forward and using the ball after the defenders have won it. I notice, too, a certain moodiness in Brady's football, but I'll forgive him that because he has the vital quality I seek in a midfield player. He looks up, asks, 'Where do you want it?' – and then delivers.

Lou Macari of Manchester United is another little man who stands tall with me. He's a competitor, always available to receive a pass, and he wants to score goals. He's only 5ft 5in., but he'll outjump giants.

Three players I admired deeply suffered from the same

problem: they were injury-prone – Kevin Beattie of Ipswich, John Richards of Wolves and Andy Gray, who moved from Aston Villa to Wolves for £1.5 million in September 1979. Beattie is a marvellous athlete, international class at left-back or as a central defender, and is able to jump above the cross-bar to head goals – but boiling chip pans spill over him, his cartilages keep failing and we've never seen him long enough at his best. Richards was a good finisher, quick, and he lived right, but injuries robbed him of pace and I don't think we ever saw him fulfil his real potential. Gray was a striker I would have bought two years before Villa made him available, but he represented too great a risk when he finally appeared on the transfer list. Brian and I discussed his outside interests; he was part owner of a nightclub and we didn't approve of that – but our main objection was that he appeared to have become susceptible to injury. Some players are, and we try to steer clear of them.

Over the years I've looked at many players and wished, 'If only I could sign him!' Denis Law was one of them, Jimmy Greaves was another and so was Bobby Moore. I liked Billy Bremner at his best and his Leeds United teammate Johnny Giles, who was one of the most purposeful players I've seen. A midfielder I always itched to sign was less famous than them, although he played twice for England. He was Mike Bailey of Wolves, but we never came nearer to capturing him than this deadlock with manager Bill McGarry, who said, 'Sure you can have him – if you give me Roy McFarland.'

McFarland was my best signing. I say that even at the risk of seeming unfair to a lot of others. What is a good signing? It has to be measured on what you pay, what service you get and what profit can be made when selling. No two players are alike on that test. He was a steal at £24,000 from Tranmere Rovers and had only one failing that we could dig at in team meetings. McFarland was careful with his money. I used to say that he was looking for a house next door to a cash-and-carry and that it took him half an hour to put his hand in his pocket whenever he bought a drink. Sometimes I am certain he felt like socking me, but it was shrewd psychology to attack a player who was otherwise invulnerable. That always goes down well with a team.

Peter Withe also ranks among my best signings. He cost a little, gave a lot and made over £200,000 profit in a short spell. Garry Birtles cost £2,000 and would fetch today not less than £1 million. There would be no shortage of buyers because he gives such honest performances. He'll be on someone's team sheet for the rest of his life.

A good signing is not breaking transfer records but backing your judgement on a player available to everyone at a modest fee – like McFarland, Roger Davies at Worcester for £14,000, or Alan Hinton, who gave superb service at Derby for only £29,000. I pulled off an outstanding coup by paying only £750 to Nuneaton Borough for goalkeeper Les Green when I managed Burton Albion. I took him to Hartlepools in 1965 and then signed him for Derby from Rochdale for £7,000. He never missed a game for two years and during that time – and I speak as an ex-'keeper – he was the best goalkeeper in the world.

I've had more luck in assessing goalkeepers and strikers than any other positions. If I don't know 'keepers then I ought to pack up football, and thirteen years between the posts also taught me about strikers. I've identified the outstanding ones immediately – right from the day that I first saw Brian Clough.

CHAPTER 21

PROBLEMS... AND SUCCESSES

Brian plays hell with everybody. It's in his nature and no one is spared; not me or his family, or trainers or players. We shrug off his criticisms, but, now and again, he runs up against people who aren't accustomed to these outbursts and who refuse to tolerate them. He found such a resistance movement on Forest's committee after a press conference in Sweden.

It was in October 1979, before the second leg of a European Cup match against the Swedish champions Oesters Vaexjoe. I was with him; he talked controversially but in a normal tone. We know from experience how reporters react to the sniff of a big story but there was no rushing to the phones after this conference. The sensational impact of his comments only became apparent when these words appeared in print:

I've been having a running battle with Forest's committee from the day I arrived. If they don't think that Peter Taylor and I are handling their affairs to the best of our ability, I suggest they get someone else. If they think anyone else can pay for a stand worth £2.5 million and produce sides that win leagues for pay of less than £30,000 a year, I wish they would give me the secret.

If they wish to shake hands and part company, they can do so with pleasure. We've been thinking of doing it for ages because, at this stage of our careers, Peter and I don't need any hassle. If the committee want hassle, let them have it with somebody else. I've been here nearly five years and it has been a pleasant stay, but I am quite capable of finding employment elsewhere.

My contribution to the discussion was a remark on how, as at Derby County, success changes directors for the worse. I said, 'We are doing the job in exactly the same way as when we arrived, but we are now being questioned about the methods that got us success in the first place.' Brian picked up this theme by saying, 'I've never been in love with directors. Our chairman, Stuart Dryden, is fantastic, but he is outnumbered at the club and in football generally.' And then he followed with the words which – taken out of context and projected in large type – incensed the committee. 'Unfortunately, the game attracts a certain percentage of people who are nobodies in their own walk of life and want to become somebodies through football. They are welcome to do that, but not on my back. Let them earn their own corn.' It was the word 'nobodies' that wounded and offended to the extent that even the chairman, usually a staunch supporter, complained, 'I'm sorry that Brian has aired the situation in such unfortunate terms.'

I was amazed that this storm in a tea cup was still raging a fortnight later; to me, it was just Brian being his usual, provocative self and needling people for the fun of it. Neither of us imagined that the outcome would be a committee meeting that could easily have ended with our departure from Forest. The two of us left the meeting for half an hour while I talked earnestly to Brian, arguing, 'Look, we either finish here and now or you go back inside and apologise to them. They're upset to a man; they've said so and you can see it. They're not ordering you to apologise but it's clear that they'll settle for one as the way to save face.'

He was het up but, in the end, saw sense and apologised profusely: 'It has been established beyond a shadow of doubt that what I said in Sweden was unbefitting the manager of a successful club. I bitterly regret what I said, and feel relieved that it's all over.' Mr Dryden attended our next pre-match press conference in Europe, which was held at Pitești in Romania a few weeks later. He didn't say more than a couple of words but, as always, acted as a balancing factor.

I was upset by the six-month prison sentence imposed on Mr Dryden in January 1980 after he had been convicted by a jury on four charges of dishonestly obtaining money from the Post Office while he was the sub-postmaster of Ruddington village. The sentence was suspended on appeal and, I felt, the case was put into perspective by being likened to 'an expenses fiddle', but it was bad for the reputation of Nottingham Forest and a blow to the partnership. I'm sure that Brian, who was in court almost throughout the seven-day trial, felt the same way.

We liked Stuart Dryden and admired the quiet dignity with which he carried out his duties through what must have been a crushing year for him. He was under investigation and suspicion, and everyone in Nottingham knew that Forest's chairman had to answer criminal charges. Some people thought him a weak character who was dominated by Brian and myself, but that wasn't so. Stuart knew how to handle us and, when we needed putting in our place, how to do it in a nice way. He had complete faith in us, he treated us with respect, and he got the best out of us – which is how it should be between chairman and management.

Brian and I were both distressed that, while on bail pending appeal against his sentence, he was turned away from the team's charter plane to Barcelona. He wasn't entitled to travel because of a committee decision to limit the number of officials in the party, but we would have liked him to see Forest follow the European Cup by taking the Super Cup in February 1980.

The magnificent Camp Nou stadium was packed with a 90,000 crowd blowing horns and beating drums. Barcelona's fans believed that our 1–0 lead from the first leg was not enough and they went wild when the scores were levelled after only twenty-eight minutes. Frankie Gray brought down Allan Simonsen, the little Dane who was a former European Footballer of the Year. A penalty was awarded and the Brazilian Carlos Roberto side-footed it past Peter Shilton.

That's the point where many away sides would crumble in Europe, but we hit back with a goal. John Robertson's corner just before half-time was flicked on by Larry Lloyd and headed in by Kenny Burns – and, as an away goal, that was worth double should Barcelona score again to square the aggregate. They didn't, though. We held on at 1–1 for our fifteenth consecutive unbeaten match in Europe, a result that put Forest's name on yet another piece of silverware. We never foresaw, however, that the club's trophy cabinet was about to lose the prize we had started to regard as our personal property – the League Cup.

Almost everyone tipped us to beat Wolverhampton Wanderers in the 1980 final at Wembley, but the first hint that things might go wrong was the suspension of Larry Lloyd for collecting twenty disciplinary points. He was banned for one match, which happened to be the final – a punishment disproportionate to his offences, as the disciplinary committee admitted by almost apologising to Larry when passing sentence.

David Needham replaced him and was then the blameless victim of a mix-up with Peter Shilton over a long ball from the Wolves midfielder Peter Daniel. A shout from a distance of eighteen yards can't be heard in the din at Wembley, so Needham didn't know that Shilton had called for the ball and was racing up behind him to gather it. Shilton arrived just as Needham was chesting the ball, the pair of them collided and the ball rolled away towards our goal. Andy Gray, the £1.5 million Scottish striker, tucked it away to win the Cup for Wolves.

Brian and I felt in despair after that defeat, yet we were on the heights again by the following Wednesday after winning 3–1 in East Germany against Dynamo Berlin. It was the quarter-final of the European Cup and we had lost the first leg at home, which is usually fatal, but I was encouraged by the nervousness of the young German team. They were wilting under the strain of being favourites. They had won at Nottingham against all expectations and were worrying about what we, as European Cup holders, might do to them in return. The Friedrich-Ludwig-Jahn-Sportpark, where we played, is alongside the Berlin Wall and the walk from the dressing rooms to the pitch is about 100 yards, the longest I've encountered. I watched Dynamo set out on this trek and crowed with delight to Brian, 'Look at them, they're like zombies. If only there were a Ladbrokes here, I'd get a bet on.'

Trevor Francis had been pulled aside by Brian before the match; he was hunched in his tracksuit top, shivering in the bitter wind. 'You look like a ninepenny rabbit, Trevor,' said Brian, but not in an unkindly way. 'Now where would you like to play?' 'Up front,' said Trevor stoutly, and justified his choice by scoring twice, including the first goal which levelled the aggregate. A penalty by John Robertson was our other goal.

The committee were still celebrating as I warned, 'Now to get the best out of Francis, we must balance the team with yet another costly signing.' Our enormous expenditure on wages and transfers caused some tensions between ourselves and the committee, because of Forest's unique place as the only private club in the league. Should anything go wrong, all the club's debts would become the personal responsibility of the 200 members. They could be asked to find more than £10,000 each.

It was only sensible to change Forest into a limited liability company, like the other ninety-one clubs. The process is a lengthy one but the members were willing to go through with it. The transfer from club to company is undoubtedly the most far-reaching innovation of our time at Nottingham, but we also made considerable strides in tackling hooliganism.

Brian's campaign against obscene chanting was followed by a programme black-list of convicted hooligans, complete with their addresses, their fines and their court costs. A voucher system of ticket distribution was used to keep out the notorious Manchester United fans, and Forest's secretary Ken Smales stated the club policy in unmistakable terms, 'We are determined to make this ground a decent place to bring women and children to watch soccer.'

So we were disgusted when, after all our efforts to improve crowd behaviour, Arsenal's goalkeeper Pat Jennings was struck in the arm by a dart thrown from the Trent End terraces. It was a wicked, cowardly assault; had Pat turned round, he could have been blinded. The only good thing about this incident in December 1979 was the indignation of our supporters, who seized the seventeen-year-old culprit and handed him over to the police. The magistrates jailed him for six months and Forest banned him for life.

As an old goalkeeper, I'm appalled at the modern readiness to hurl missiles at the helpless target of the man between the sticks. Anfield is one of the worst grounds for it. Liverpool fans don't even wait for the kick-off; they start bombarding as soon as Peter Shilton and myself go out to inspect the goalmouths. We've been showered and hit at both ends with coins, fruit and beer cans. I'm not being brave in saying that the crowd will never stop us from examining conditions in both goals. It's a job that has to be done. What a commentary on today's sportsmanship that we should have to do it while keeping our heads down!

CHAPTER 22

MADRID

We drove in silence to our second European Cup final; the players hardly glanced out of the coach windows as the road from our hideaway hotel wound between the mountains to join the motorway into Madrid, thirty-three miles away.

'A good sign,' I whispered to Brian. 'They're really concentrating.' Usually, we move along the aisle and talk to the lads during journeys but this time we left them with their thoughts. They had plenty to think about and so had we – defeat by Hamburg, starring Kevin Keegan, in this 1980 final would put Forest out of European competition for the following season and memories were still fresh of another muted coach ride only ten weeks previously after our defeat by Wolves in the League Cup final at Wembley. Peter Shilton's collision with David Needham when running out unnecessarily for a long cross had cost us the chance of completing a hat-trick of League Cup final victories and, worse still, had denied us the place in the UEFA Cup that now goes automatically to the League Cup winners. Because of inconsistent league form, Forest could stay in Europe only by retaining the European Cup.

The journey that led us to Real Madrid's tiered stadium on a chilly May evening had stretched through Sweden, Romania, East Germany and Holland over eight months, starting with a 3–1 aggregate win against Oesters Vaexjoe who, although more enterprising than the Swedes from Malmö, were a class below us. Argeş Piteşti, the Romanian champions, were eliminated on a 4–1 aggregate despite fielding several players who seemed inclined to kick us out of Europe. One of them, Mihai Zamfir, was sent off at Nottingham after fouling Tony Woodcock and Garry Birtles, and his clubmates conceded thirty-one free kicks – five of them in the first four minutes – when we went to Piteşti for the second leg. I remember the stadium filling with spectators in the morning for an afternoon kick-off and the muddle over seating that meant chairman Stuart Dryden had to watch standing up; not that Stuart cared, he would have been happy standing behind the goal. Most of all, I remember our fifth-minute goal from a corner by John Robertson that was chested down by Larry Lloyd and shot in by Ian Bowyer.

Early goals are essential in two-legged games and one in our next European match, a stabbing shot by Trevor Francis in the fifteenth minute, wiped out Dynamo Berlin's 1–0 lead from the first leg and undermined their morale. We had heard horror stories about the obstacles awaiting us in East Germany but none of them was true; the Dynamo club treated us courteously and pleasantly and their football was clean and honest. However, tactically speaking, Iron Curtain sides tend to play as they live – with a system which suffocates individual flair. It was a pity because Dynamo had players I would like to see in English football, notably Hans-Jürgen Riediger, the blond centre-forward who scored their break-away goal in Nottingham.

Our next opponents were Ajax Amsterdam, who had won the European Cup in successive years, 1971–73, in the great days of Johan Cruyff and Johan Neeskens. The fame of Ajax produced intense media activity and we feared that the home leg of this semi-final might be looming too large in the minds of the players, so we did something that few clubs would risk on the eve of a big game – we gave them Tuesday off. Some went shopping or to the races, I went to Scarborough and Brian had a day at home; we all returned refreshed.

Only Ruud Krol, now the sweeper and captain, survived from the famous Ajax side and he couldn't turn the tide at Nottingham. We were cultured that night, always in control and treated unjustly by the scoreline, because we were worth more than our 2–0 win through a shot by Trevor Francis and a penalty by John Robertson.

The second leg began unpromisingly; we were driven to the wrong hotel in Amsterdam, then directed to the wrong training ground and next criticised by the main Dutch newspapers for staging our pre-match press conference in a bar. News, not venues, are what press conferences are about; the Dutch couldn't complain on that score because topics flowed and they got plenty of copy. Nevertheless, they seemed to disapprove of the setting as frivolous, so I wonder what would have been written if we had been spotted that evening, and on the night before the match, leading the players on a tour of the red-light district. Our hotel was near the central railway station and not far from the notorious Oudezijds Voorburgwal, which is better known as Canal Street. Every alley and gabled house seems to offer a sex shop, a porno cinema, a bar, or girls in windows eyeing the strollers for possible custom. 'Don't stop, keep walking,' we shouted over our shoulders, but on Tuesday, the eve of the game, we did stop. We had found a pub that was spotless and quiet and run by a woman who worked in the clubhouse bar at the Ajax ground; we took the players in, ordered up several rounds of beers, listened to the jukebox and stayed for half an hour chatting to the locals. Unorthodox, certainly – but where's the harm? The lads had enjoyed the break and a laugh, they slept well and everyone was in the right shape next evening, because a few beers never hurt a footballer. Only Trevor Francis was out of form; moves broke down around him and Garry Birtles had to carry the attack single-handed.

I lectured Trevor at half-time: 'You're not holding the ball and making runs to relieve the pressure on the defence. You give the impression of waiting to be chopped down, but I've not seen one filthy tackle and I don't think there are going to be any. So get on with it!'

We lost 1–0, which meant entry to the final on a 2–1 aggregate, but our lead was almost lost by Trevor breaking off the end of our wall and deflecting a free kick towards Peter Shilton's left-hand post, crying in dismay, 'It's in, Shilts!' But it wasn't – Peter dived for a superb save and sent us safely to neutral Madrid.

We flew out a man short because Stan Bowles had gone absent without leave, which sharpened the point of a joke that had been going the rounds of Nottingham. It began with Brian supposedly addressing Bowles, 'Hey, young man,' a greeting that has become a Clough catchphrase. The story continued, 'Hey, young man. I'm not worried about your gambling, I'm not worried about your private life, but I am worried that you have a very bad record for not turning up.'

To which Bowles answers, 'But, boss, I'm terrified of flying,' and receives the reply, 'Young man, do as I do. Get drunk and take a Valium.'

There was more meat in the story than, perhaps, the inventor realised because Brian went through a couple of years of avoiding plane trips. A rough flight (to Russia, I think) frightened him and, although he has now overcome his nerves, I remember him ashen-faced and fortifying himself with brandy on a short hop from Guernsey to East Midlands Airport. Coincidentally, too, Stan Bowles is on tranquillisers and came to me in alarm after being selected for a random dope test at Derby. 'I take Valium,' he said, so I told him, 'We all do at times but it's not on the FA's list of banned drugs.'

Bad fliers – and Sammy Chapman was the jumpiest – get no mercy from us. We fill them with pills and fasten their seat belts; when a team flies, everyone in it flies. There is no opting out.

The problem with Bowles, though, was deeper than a fear of flying. He walked out because he wanted a transfer and I understood his feelings; he wasn't being picked for away matches and, although there had been no open row, he was fairly sure that Brian didn't rate him either as a player or a person. He asked to see me at Forest's ground shortly before the kick-off of John Robertson's testimonial match against Leicester City, saying, 'If I can't get picked for a benefit game, what am I doing here? I'd better have a transfer.'

I advised him, 'Go away and count to ten. We're only a fortnight from the European Cup final and, even though it might not seem so now, you are in contention for a place.'

He took no notice. 'I can't stick it here, I'm off,' he said, and left the ground without staying for the match. He didn't report for the club's flight to Majorca, where the team rested before the final, and he didn't turn up for the trip to Madrid.

I liked Bowles. His talent will be remembered when hundreds of more sterling characters are forgotten, but I finished with him over his foolishness in not deferring his transfer request until the season ended and throwing away a chance to show his skills to millions in the European Cup final.

The loss of Francis and Bowles forced tactical changes on us in Madrid, as well as a gamble on Gary Mills who, at eighteen and a half, was the youngest European Cup finalist since Brian Kidd of Manchester United in 1968. Mills has pace, having run in the All-England Schools' 100 metres final; his background is right as the son of a former Northampton Town professional, Roley Mills, and I think he is the only boy who has been capped at both soccer and Rugby Union by England Schools. Gary played for our reserves while still at school and I remember him, as a fifteen-year-old, transforming a pre-season match against a non-league side; he switched to centre-forward and licked a defence of grown men. So Mills was good, but rather young for a European

Cup final, especially in a tired team. Weariness also worried us – Brian and I knew that the players were not fully rested even after a week in Majorca and we didn't want to share the fate of Arsenal in the 1980 Cup Winners' Cup final when they lost to Valencia on penalties after drawing 0–0. Arsenal could play Valencia ten times and win nine of the matches, but not at the end of a long season. Fatigue prevented Arsenal from showing their true form and it threatened us because, including pre-season fixtures, the final would be our seventy-ninth match.

Happily, the build-up had been good. Brian and I had brainwashed the team for two days at our hotel in the Sierra de Guadarrama, preparing them for the danger of the match turning brutal because so much depended on the result. We had to win to stay in Europe, Keegan had to win to become the first player earning victory medals with two different European Cup finalists, Liverpool and Hamburg, and the Germans – who can be just as physical as the British – had to win as insurance against the probability of losing the Bundesliga championship. In fact, three days later, Bayern Munich took the title from Hamburg.

We strung five men across midfield to weather the storm bound to burst upon us from the kick-off. We have never fielded a tighter formation, yet Forest took the lead in the twentieth minute when John Robertson scored after his first run at Hamburg's renowned right-back Manny Kaltz. The shot went in off the post and I hoped we could stay in front; I knew that victory by a big score was improbable and had forecast to the press, 'One goal will be enough for us.'

I had seen Hamburg twice, firstly at Stuttgart with Brian and then by myself at Leverkusen where they lost 2–1 on the Saturday before the final. They failed to impress me, as I told the team meeting: 'Horst Hrubesch, their top scorer, can head the ball and is strong and brave, but I don't rate him because he has nothing downstairs and needs half an hour to turn round. On top of that, he got a bad knock last Saturday. Kevin Keegan is tiring, as he usually does towards the end of a season. Their goalkeeper, Kargus, isn't worth two bob and I can't see a tactical pattern in the team. Hamburg are there to be taken, especially if we get at Kaltz. He's their strength but he doesn't look good when attacked.'

I took the players on the pitch about an hour before the kick-off, as I do wherever we play, and then examined both goalmouths with Peter Shilton. I kept it secret that the doctor was waiting in the dressing room with a painkilling injection for Peter. He had pulled a calf muscle, the first injury of that nature in his career, before starting his training routine at the hotel. The cancellation of a workout troubled Peter, who kept saying, 'I'll have to handle the ball, I have to feel it every day.'

We told him firmly, 'Not today, you won't. It's ice packs for you and no exercises.' He insisted, however, on the day of the match, 'No matter how it hurts, I'll have to handle.' Jimmy Montgomery, our veteran reserve 'keeper, was told to stand by for a possible first appearance of the season, although Peter felt confident about playing with the aid of painkillers.

While the injection was administered, Brian and I watched the other players. Larry Lloyd was cocky, as always; a team needs that buoyant type to balance the quiet ones who tuck themselves away, such as Garry Birtles, Viv Anderson and Frank Gray.

I never fail to be fascinated by the atmosphere in a dressing room before a match. Brian and I hover and observe, conferring briefly, sensing who needs lifting and who ought to be left alone, sometimes leaving the dressing room for a minute through knowing that there are times when the team needs us and others when we are better out of the way. We have no set pattern except that we rarely enter the dressing room at home matches until a quarter of an hour before the kick-off. Concentrated impact is the name of our pre-match game, and the effect can wear off if delivered too early.

We weren't far short of needing a pep talk ourselves as the final developed into a long, defensive night for us. We knew there was little hope of adding to our lead; indeed, it was the eighty-seventh minute before a long run by Birtles gave us a chance to make it 2–0. He was tired, though, and not alert to the defender coming to dispossess him. 'I wasn't aware of him,' Garry told me. 'I was thinking only that it was a certain goal if I could take the ball round the 'keeper.'

'You didn't need those sort of trimmings,' I replied. 'All it required was a simple, left-foot shot.'

Hamburg withdrew Holger Hieronymus at half-time and sent on Hrubesch, whose damaged ankle was full of painkiller. He won some balls in the air but looked unfit, naturally enough, and the most dangerous second-half shots came from the defenders; Kaltz, who hit the post with a magnificent shot, and Nogly, whose twenty-yarder was knocked away by Shilton for a corner.

Shilton had made two excellent saves in the first half, plunging left to stop shots by Magath and Milewski. The half-volley by Milewski was a chance set up for him by Keegan, and Peter, who always discusses every save with me, said afterwards, 'That was the best one, the opening that came from Kevin heading down. I had a clear view of their other attempts, but that one was a bit late.'

Brian had left us for the press conference in Real Madrid's gymnasium, where he gave Branko Zebec, Hamburg's manager, a hug and a kiss before saying ecstatically, 'This is probably the greatest moment of my career. I cannot remember ever being so emotionally involved in a game; it seemed to go on for hours instead of only ninety minutes. I've not seen a team apply itself better for many years. Shilton, Burns, Lloyd spring to mind but it's pointless mentioning names because everybody concerned with Nottingham Forest has won the European Cup. We gave Hamburg a lesson in application, determination, dedication and pride, all the good things we don't hear enough about and that are taken for granted in English football. We had no option but to defend, and if you have to defend then you must do it well. We did it well. We weren't lucky, we were good.'

How irritating that our joy was soon to be marred by a wrangle with some of the players over the after-match arrangements. A sumptuous buffet had been provided in the city for the players' wives, club staff and close friends of Forest, including the Clough and Taylor families, but we whisked the players back to our remote hotel. Our bus left the stadium an hour after the final whistle with the fifteen players, trainer Jimmy Gordon, physiotherapist Tony Verity, club secretary Ken Smales, Brian and myself. A meal awaited us and the bar was kept open for those who wanted to sit up drinking; I wasn't one of them because I went to bed at 1.10 a.m. and left the grumblers to it. They wanted to go into Madrid to see their wives and didn't think much of our view: 'It's a European Cup final, not a social outing. When we go as a team, we must leave as a team and not with players scattered all over the place, thirty-three miles away. Besides, the season is officially over when we land at East Midlands on Thursday and then you can spend as much time with your wives as you want.'

Celebrations, as I've said earlier, are always low in our priorities and particularly so on that night in Madrid where bigger things were on our minds – like a new three-year contract with Forest, an offer to manage Barcelona, and the proposed sale of Trevor Francis to Barcelona for £1.5 million. Two officials from the Barcelona club came to the hotel to open negotiations for Francis even though aware that he might not be fit for five or six months. We had met one of them, a rich hotelier, during the Super Cup; he spoke good English and turned the conversation to management, asking, 'Could you two do in Spain what you've done in England? If so, the job is yours. Why not fly back on Friday and talk it over with us? You see, we have no manager except for Helenio Herrera who is into his sixties and only a stop-gap; he would depart immediately if you came. Look, we have a contract here for the signing of Diego Maradona from Argentina, so think what an attack you would have with Francis alongside him.'

We thanked him while pointing out, 'You're about three hours too late. We've just agreed terms with Forest for new three-year contracts and, although nothing is signed, cannot go back on our word.'

The offer and the new contract followed by victory in the final combined to put Brian in an expansive mood on the coach ride back to Madrid's airport. He lounged in his seat and asked me, 'Pete, tell me what we've won and in how long. What is it, about four years? Two European Cups, a championship, two League Cups – has anyone ever done as much in such a short time?'

I said, 'I know it started with the Anglo-Scottish Cup against Orient at the back-end of 1976. We've won so much that I can't remember everything, except that we've been in five finals and won four of them.'

A check in the records at home showed I was wrong about the finals. We have played in seven, winning six. The full list of achievements starts on 15 December 1976 when we beat Orient 4–0 in the second leg of the Anglo-Scottish Cup, our first final. After that, in order, Forest won promotion from the Second Division in season 1976–77, the League Cup in 1978 and the 1977–78 League Championship, the FA Charity Shield in 1978, the League Cup in 1979, the European Cup in 1979, the Super Cup in 1980 and, lastly, the European Cup again. We had played finals against Orient, Liverpool, Southampton, Malmö, Barcelona, Wolves and Hamburg, losing only to Wolves.

Where do we go from there? 'On and on,' said Brian. How typical of him that, even as thousands of supporters gathered to welcome us home from Madrid, he should be considering our placing of fifth in the First Division and saying to me, 'You know, we ought to have had a better season.'

CHAPTER 23

THE MAGIC FORMULA

'Taylor finds the players, Clough gives them the gee up' is how fans might describe the chemistry of our partnership. But it's more complex than that and, even after fifteen years together, I cannot put a finger on the precise formula. The basic element is togetherness; we're always picking up each other's thoughts and finishing each other's sentences; we're a twosome speaking as one.

If there is anything that we have taught football management, it is the importance of being independent, positive and decisive. The game is full of vacillating men but, with us, a decision is followed by instant action. We brook no interference. Our record guarantees some other club waiting round the corner, so we can be our own men and mean it when we tell employers at the start, 'We've explained how we manage. If you approve of that now, don't complain afterwards.'

Tony Woodcock told a German magazine last winter that we never talk tactics when, in fact, we hardly talk about anything else. Tactics are not diagrams and little arrows on a blackboard, but blends and formations and signings and football as a whole. We discuss football all day and often long into the night; Brian sits at home until the small hours watching videotaped matches.

We're always trying to find answers, but the one we never find is why we're so successful together in the game when we're so different outside it. Brian enjoys dining out, company and public attention; I prefer the peace of walks with my wife along the banks of Rutland Lake. He plays squash every day; I go to the races, although the pleasure is being spoiled by knots of fans peering over my shoulder whenever I place a bet.

I'm a bit shy of strangers. I've stopped shopping in Nottingham because there's no relief from being recognised, engaged in conversation and asked for autographs. The celebrity treatment, and I understand that it's part of the job, is a considerable nuisance at the races, where I'm often betting on inside information with money from friends who trust me to obtain a fair price.

A couple of years ago I roped in the family and two men from Forest to spread £500 in small bets at Southwell for a northern contact. It's the best way to avoid arousing suspicion in the bookies' ring. An owner called me at home, asking only, 'Going to Wetherby tomorrow?' No elaboration was required. I turned up in my scouting disguise of cap and glasses, acted a bit gormless and spread £400 on his horse without the bookies twigging a coup. It won and the lowest price we got was 3–1. My best day at the races was when I won £1,500 after starting with next to nothing. Now fame works against me, and I dislike people trying to find out what I'm backing and for how much.

I'm glad that my children have been protected from the limelight, because life can be difficult for the families of football managers. I remember Don Revie, when manager of Leeds United, telling me of the Saturday afternoon when he found his son Duncan alone, huddled against a tree outside Villa Park. The boy's coach home had gone. Duncan had deliberately missed it, because Leeds had lost and he knew that his ride back from Birmingham would be like running the gauntlet.

'He was only eleven years old and the game was already making his life a misery,' said Don. 'I knew I would have to get him away from Leeds and supporters and football. And that's why I sent him as a boarder to Repton School, although it broke my heart because we're such a close family.'

I've kept my family away from football, as far as possible, and yet I know that the game has caused them pain. They never seem to understand how public appreciation of an equal partnership isn't split down the middle, like salaries and bonuses.

All partnerships, whether in marriage or business, produce problems. The sharing of fame is ours and I've often had relatives asking, 'Why does Brian Clough get all the publicity, not you? It's your team, too, isn't it?' I'm not particularly worried about this. I'm certainly not resentful of Brian's renown, but I sometimes wonder why he never says to Bell's whisky, for instance, when they're handing out Manager of the Month awards, 'You'll have to present an extra gallon bottle. There are two of us.'

Brian will often say of himself, 'I'm only the shop window, Peter is the goods at the back,' but it's only to pacify me and is not the concrete acknowledgement that some of my family expect. I tell them, 'Look, the people who employ us and the players know my contribution, which is all that matters to me.'

Brian and I are both family men; it's one of the few things we have in common off the field. He is always glad to get home to Barbara and the three children, and I remember the night he celebrated our first League Cup victory by placing the trophy on top of the television set while they all sat around eating fish and chips.

It's not easy to raise a family properly in professional football, because the job calls for seven-day-a-week involvement, absences from home, a phone that never stops ringing even on free evenings and frequent uprootings. For instance, we have lived in Coventry, Middlesbrough, the Potteries, Burton, Hartlepools, Derby, Brighton and now Nottingham. My family followed without hesitation until I proposed leaving Brighton to rejoin Brian at Forest; then they had doubts. They knew that I missed the close contact with big football in the Midlands and the north and that I missed Brian and the old, successful partnership, but Lilian worried about the risk to my health. She felt that my heart attack at Derby might have been caused by the stress of working with a character as forceful and unpredictable as Brian; she didn't want a recurrence.

I've been lucky in Lilian, Wendy and Philip. I'm proud of their honesty and delighted with their support through some years of turmoil. When I'm in the news, they get dragged in as well. Now Philip is nice and equable and will smooth over difficulties with my critics, but Wendy is fiery and wants to hit back, although I tell her, 'It doesn't matter what other people think, but only what we think.' One of Lilian's greatest assets is her detachment from football. After a bad result, the last thing a manager needs is an opinionated wife, but I have the relief of knowing that I can rely on the same calm homecoming whether we've won 6–0 or been knocked out of the European Cup.

The 1–0 defeat at home by Dynamo Berlin in the European Cup quarter-finals last season was the most disappointing result of my career; I needed time afterwards to collect my thoughts. I switched on the TV highlights of the match for a second chance to study the faults in our finishing and the type of chances that had been offered to us. Lilian came in with a sandwich and a cup of tea, and I had to call her before she would watch the football. If I asked, 'Who are we playing on Saturday?' she wouldn't know.

Unfortunately, the game is full of wives who are only too ready to sound off. I'm thinking, particularly, of players' wives and I'm annoyed when their opinions are relayed to me. Football is a man's game and I'm not interested in what women think about it. I never again want to hear the phrase, 'My wife thought...' Brian feels the same way. Why, he doesn't even want to hear what an ex-professional like Jimmy Hill thinks. I enjoy BBC's *Match of the Day* and I don't agree with Brian that Jimmy is a headmaster, lecturing and boring the viewers.

Brian, as I've mentioned earlier, was offered Hill's old job by London Weekend. He didn't take it, possibly through an awareness of his own drawbacks. I can't imagine Brian submitting scripts to anyone or smiling cheerfully when they are thrown back to him for redrafting. Has the producer been born who can order Brian Clough around year after year?

The speculation about Brian leaving football for TV or

politics is rubbish. I know he was approached only in 1979 about standing as Labour's parliamentary candidate at Loughborough. He is famous, eloquent and might even win, but he has neither the diplomacy nor the background that a politician needs.

It's important to understand about Brian and myself that we're only football people. Physical people, not academic, clerical or patient. On top of that, Brian suffers from terrible insecurity. He is supposed to be the booster when, in fact, he's the one who needs boosting. You'll never see him alone, which is the most obvious way that he betrays his lack of confidence.

A succession of blows contributed to his other hidden fears; for instance, although probably the brightest and certainly the most successful of the Clough children, Brian was the only one to fail the 11-plus examination. He was hurt again by being cast aside so hastily by England and he still feels the knee injury that destroyed his dream of First Division football. The stormy finish at Derby County left a scar and then, just when recovering his old buoyancy, the sack from Leeds United plunged him into fresh despair.

It's been one long happy ending since the restoration of our partnership and we have now signed new contracts tying us to Forest until 1983. Both of us, though, are aware that it cannot last for ever and that we must part again one day. I hope we part on a high note and on the friendliest terms, and that football will remember us as pioneers of management – the first to see that two heads are better than one.

BRIEF CHRONOLOGY OF PETER TAYLOR'S CAREER TO 1980

2 July 1928	Born in Nottingham
21 April 1945	Debut for Forest Colts, Nottingham Forest's youth team
2 July 1945	Signed for Coventry City
1 August 1955	Sold to Middlesbrough
12 June 1961	Sold to Port Vale
July 1962	Left Port Vale on a free transfer to Burton Albion
October 1962	Manager of Burton Albion
October 1965	Appointed assistant manager at Hartlepools United
May 1967	Assistant manager at Derby County

1 November 1973	Assistant manager at Brighton and Hove Albion
22 July 1974	Manager of Brighton and Hove Albion
16 July 1976	Resigned as Brighton manager and joined Clough as assistant manager of Nottingham Forest

BRIEF CHRONOLOGY
OF BRIAN CLOUGH'S
CAREER TO 1980

21 March 1935	Born in Middlesbrough
17 September 1955	Debut for Middlesbrough
14 July 1961	Sold to Sunderland
26 December 1962	Injured against Bury
2 July 1965	Sacked as Sunderland youth coach
29 October 1965	Manager of Hartlepools United
1 June 1967	Manager of Derby County
15 October 1973	Resigned from Derby County
1 November 1973	Manager of Brighton and Hove Albion
30 July 1974	Manager of Leeds United
12 September 1974	Sacked by Leeds United
6 January 1975	Manager of Nottingham Forest

ABOUT THE AUTHOR

© John Sumpter

Peter Taylor was born on 2 July 1928, one of eight children, and was raised in The Meadows, Nottingham.

Taylor had a modest goalkeeping career which began with the youth team at Nottingham Forest – the club he would one day lead to European glory. After retirement, he launched a successful managerial partnership with a centre-forward he met during his playing days at Middlesbrough: Brian Clough.

Together, the pair won seven major cups, two Football League championships, two promotions to the First Division and the FA Charity Shield. Uniquely since the Second World War, their successes were achieved with two clubs, Derby County and Nottingham Forest, turning these struggling Second Division teams into champions against all odds. Their crowning glories came in 1979 and 1980 when they won two consecutive European Cups. The partnership, which had redefined football management, ended in 1982 when Peter resigned from Nottingham Forest.

Taylor was also a manager in his own right, coaching Burton Albion, Brighton and Hove Albion and, later, Derby County.

He was married to Lilian and had two children, Wendy and Philip. He died suddenly of idiopathic pulmonary fibrosis while on holiday in Majorca in 1990.

INDEX